DISCOVERING
ABERDEEN

DISCOVERING
ABERDEEN

ANN WILLIAMS

RICHARD DREW PUBLISHING

First published by
Richard Drew Publishing Ltd 1982
20 Park Circus
Glasgow G3 6BE

ISBN 0 904002 94 2

Made and Printed in Great Britain by
William Collins Sons & Co Ltd, Glasgow

For
JANE AND JIMMY LEE

Preface

Aberdeen does not yield up its beauties as easily as Edinburgh. Many landmarks had been destroyed before the oil industry gave the excuse for further depradations. The close proximity of the old and the new is sometimes exciting, more often drab and unimaginative. The heritage of granite buildings, both public and vernacular, is often shamed by the poor use of modern materials, but the city is saved by its site between the two magnificent rivers, the Don and the Dee, by the city's inspired development of its open spaces and by the backbone of its 19th-century planning, the broad vistas of which have preserved the centre in spite of plans for stereotyped shopping precincts and urban motorways.

As well as being an international oil capital, Aberdeen remains what it always has been, the regional capital of north-east Scotland. Its fishing industry has declined, but its agricultural hinterland is rich. The roads which lead from it penetrate very different types of countryside, from the rocky coastline to the south, the mountainous scenery of Deeside, the subtler beauty of the Don's hills to the coastal plain of Buchan in the north-east. The second part of the book is not comprehensive, but it tries to give a taste of the area and to encourage further exploration. Apart from Routes 21–23 it is possible to make most of the journeys by public transport as well as by car.

I thank Antony Kamm for his help, and also Colin McLaren and the staff of the MacBean Room in Aberdeen University Library.

Contents

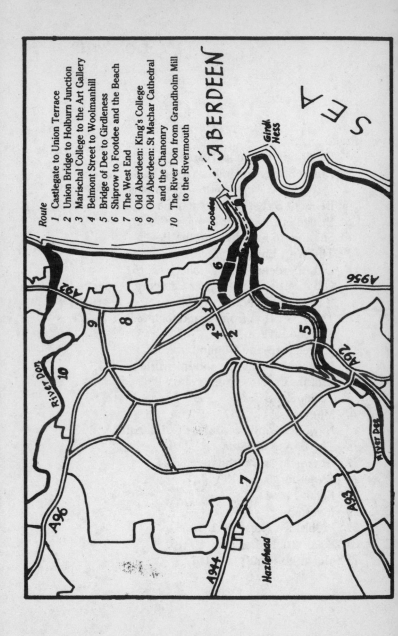

Route

ABERDEEN

SEA

Girdle Ness

Footdee

River Don

River Dee

A96

A944

A93

A92

A956

A92

A93

Hazlehead

NORTH

SEA

ABERDEEN

MORAY FIRTH

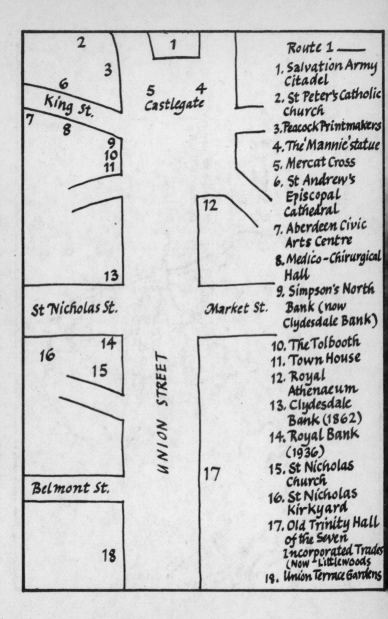

Route 1 ——

1. Salvation Army Citadel
2. St Peter's Catholic Church
3. Peacock Printmakers
4. The 'Mannie' statue
5. Mercat Cross
6. St Andrew's Episcopal Cathedral
7. Aberdeen Civic Arts Centre
8. Medico-Chirurgical Hall
9. Simpson's North Bank (now Clydesdale Bank)
10. The Tolbooth
11. Town House
12. Royal Athenaeum
13. Clydesdale Bank (1862)
14. Royal Bank (1936)
15. St Nicholas Church
16. St Nicholas Kirkyard
17. Old Trinity Hall of the Seven Incorporated Trades (now Littlewoods)
18. Union Terrace Gardens

King St.

Castlegate

St Nicholas St.

Market St.

UNION STREET

Belmont St.

CASTLEGATE TO UNION TERRACE

MANY OF ABERDEEN'S ORIGINAL LANDMARKS can be traced only in the surviving place names. The Castlegate, or way to the castle, was an open market-place. However, today, standing in the Castlegate at the foot of Union Street there is no trace of the castle itself. The hill on which it stood (on the east side behind the Salvation Army Citadel) has been levelled to carry blocks of flats. The Salvation Army Citadel, newly-cleaned, is the first of a number of Scottish baronial buildings in the city. The architect James Souttar completed it in 1896. On the north side in Chapel Court look at St Peter's Catholic Church, in which hangs a charming primitive painting of the 19th-century congregation. In the next close on the same side Peacock Printmakers have turned an old warehouse into a studio where local artists and students can produce prints.

On the south side the 19th-century tenements are sadly in bad repair; only the 18th-century building now housing a pub has not been allowed to suffer badly. Out from the buildings on an island site are the 'planestanes'. Formerly sited in front of the

Mercat Cross, they are the surviving stones of the older pavement of the Castlegate. Nearby the rectangular fountain head with the 'Mannie' statue on top has made several moves round the Castlegate before finding its present resting-place.

Cross into the centre of the Castlegate. The particularly fine Mercat Cross is built of red sandstone, the building material used in Aberdeen before granite, and was commissioned in 1686 by the Town Council from John Montgomery of Old Rayne. It has a circular arcade 21 feet in diameter and 18 feet high. Above this is a Corinthian capital with a white marble unicorn on top. Its most interesting aspect is the parapet with the Royal Arms of Scotland, the Arms of Aberdeen and relief portraits of the kings of Scotland (the last four of England too) from James I to James VII. The capitals of the pillars are decorated with animal gargoyles.

If you have time before walking up Union Street, look at some of the buildings in King Street, the broad road which goes north from the Castlegate. This street was opened up in 1801 as part of the development of the city centre. On the right is St Andrew's Episcopal Cathedral. Archibald Simpson (see Route 2 for his biography) was the architect in 1817 of the original St Andrew's Chapel. It is built in granite ashlar in the Gothic style. The porch added in 1911 does not improve the facade, and the interior has also had a number of additions. The other granite ashlar buildings on this side as far as East North Street are good examples of early-19th-century building, and were designed by John

Smith, an architect and a contemporary of Archibald Simpson.

Cross the road here and turn back towards Union Street. On the corner with West North Street is John Smith's North Church of 1828-30, now the Aberdeen Civic Arts Centre. The rectangular building has a portico supported by four Ionic columns, and a square tower surmounted by a 'tower of the winds'. This part of the street now has a unity for the buildings were designed by Smith and Simpson in consultation. No 29 King Street is the Medico-Chirurgical Hall built by Simpson in 1818-20. It has a similar portico to the Arts Centre with Ionic pillars. The buildings on either side, that on the right now the Children's Theatre and on the left the Customs and Excise Department, were added by Smith. Nos 1-5 King Street were also designed by Simpson in neo-Greek style, and this block was completed in 1836 when James Gillespie Graham added Nos 7-9 with a ground-floor arch and pilastered Doric columns above.

On the corner is Simpson's North Bank (now the Clydesdale Bank) building. This fine structure is of three storeys with a cornice at the second floor. The portico on the corner has a flat top on which stands a painted terracotta sculpture by James Giles (1801-70). It represents the Greek Earth goddess Ceres with her cornucopia, accompanied by an attractive 'British' lion. Lodge Walk, beyond the Bank, leads to the 17th-century Tolbooth. It has a three-storied square tower with corbelled battlements and a lead spire. The top of this building is really seen best from the other side of the road. Several of Aberdeen's earlier civic buildings were replaced by the Scottish baronial Town House (1868) which houses the Council Chamber and the Sheriff Court. Inside are civic portraits and a splendid circular staircase at the fork of which is Alexander Brodie's marble statue 1864 of Queen Victoria and Mary, Queen of Scots. The Charter Room of the Town House contains a rich collection of burgh records, including the first charter granted to the burgh by King William the Lion (c 1179), and Robert the Bruce's Charter of 1319 giving the 'Freedom Lands' of Aberdeen.

On the opposite side of the street retrace your steps once more to the Castlegate by the fountain heads and look across at the Royal Athenaeum, a neo-classical building designed by Archibald Simpson. Originally planned to house a circulating library, it eventually became a restaurant until it was burnt down in 1973. It was then rebuilt to its former plan and used as offices. The Castle Street side of the building has six arched windows on the ground floor and an arched entrance. Above these are three two-storied windows with an architrave over them. The side of this block is in Union Street. Also designed by Archibald Simpson, the building is of four storeys and an attic, with eleven windows at each level, the centre five projecting and with a classical swagged design. The ground-floor windows, originally arched, have been altered.

Pause a moment to look up the length of Union Street. Planned in the early 19th century, it was an outstandingly imaginative piece of town planning. The Hill of St Katharine on the left was levelled, and the street was constructed on arches over the old Putachie and Denburn which flowed down to the harbour. The arches are hidden except at Union Bridge. Walk to where Market Street on the left and St Nicholas Street on the right intersect the street. In the eastern corner of St Nicholas Street is the 1862 Renaissance-style building of the Clydesdale Bank, the work of the architect James Matthews. The 1936 Royal Bank by Jenkins and Marr follows the tradition of Corinthian columns on a granite facade.

Continue along Union Street until on the right you come to the colonnade in front of St Nicholas Church. Completed in 1830 by the city architect John Smith, it is said to be a modified form of a plan by Decimus Burton. It is composed of a series of Ionic columns 147 feet long with fine cast-iron railings. The gateway leads into St Nicholas Kirkyard. This is a splendid place for the collection of tombstone inscriptions and funerary monuments. On the west wall there is an interesting range of 17th- and early-18th-century tombstones, some in Italianate style with elegant inscriptions. The later memorials are also of interest. One is 'In Memory of Captain William Penny, Aberdeen, Artic (sic) discoverer who assisted in the Franklin Search Expeditions of 1850 and 1851'.

St Nicholas Kirk is set back on rising ground. Dedicated to the patron saint of the city, it is in fact two churches joined together. The original church was probably destroyed in 1153 in a fire which also ruined much of the city. The great door in front of you leads into the oldest existing part, the crossing of the older church. The south transept, Drum's Aisle, has an effigy of Sir Alexander Drum (d 1457). The north transept, called Collison's Aisle, is of the 17th century, although the north window, the 'Faire Windo' with its lead tracery dates from 1518. This side contains memorials to early provosts of the burgh. The tower was burnt in 1874 and was replaced with a Gothic structure. The East Church, designed by Archibald Simpson, has four needlework panels, dated c1660, worked by Mary Jamesone, the daughter of George Jamesone, and there are numbered wooden box pews. Under this part is the old St Mary's Chapel, 'Our Ladye of Pittye her vault', a rare survival of Aberdeen's medieval past.

The West Church was built in 1751-55. The architect was James Gibb, a native of Aberdeen, but more famous for his London churches, St Martin-in-the-Fields and St Mary le-Strand. He died before the building was completed. It is in Renaissance style, comprising five bays with aisles and is built of sandstone. The ceiling is barrel vaulted with groin vaulted aisles and Doric arcades. The pulpit is of the same period. The east gallery with the canopy is the 'Council's Loft' used for the 'kirking' of the Lord Provost and Council.

Return to Union Street and walk up towards Union Bridge. The modern facades of the shops on the south side have spoilt the appearance of this section of the street. On the left Littlewoods' store has engulfed the old Trinity Hall of the Seven Incorporated Trades, although parts of it can still be seen in the upstairs restaurant. On the north side the open work of the bridge can be seen overlooking Union Terrace Gardens, the landscaped valley of the Denburn which now runs underground. The Union Bridge was designed by Thomas Fletcher in 1805, following the ideas of Thomas Telford. A century later it was widened with the parapet with leopard finials designed by Sir William Kelly. Union Gardens are a pleasant relaxing place in which to end this walk.

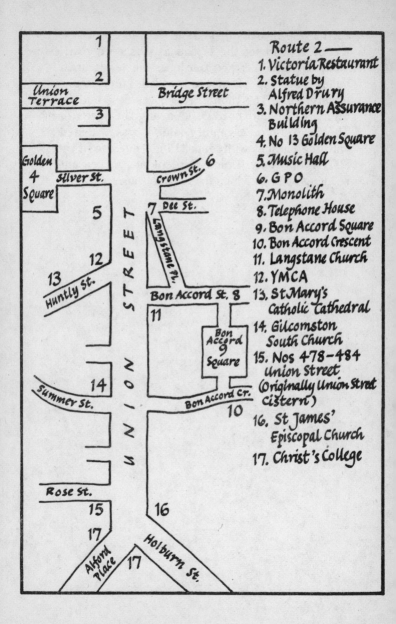

Route 2 ———
1. Victoria Restaurant
2. Statue by Alfred Drury
3. Northern Assurance Building
4. No 13 Golden Square
5. Music Hall
6. GPO
7. Monolith
8. Telephone House
9. Bon Accord Square
10. Bon Accord Crescent
11. Langstane Church
12. YMCA
13. St Mary's Catholic Cathedral
14. Gilcomston South Church
15. Nos 478–484 Union Street (Originally Union Street Cistern)
16. St James' Episcopal Church
17. Christ's College

Route 2

UNION BRIDGE TO HOLBURN JUNCTION

TAKE UP THIS WALK FROM UNION BRIDGE IN the middle of Union Street. Stand on the northern side of the bridge looking down on Union Street Gardens. The building on the right-hand side, now the Victoria Restaurant, is a granite ashlar building by Archibald Simpson. On the Union Terrace Gardens side you can see the full seven storeys, while the Union Street facade is only three storeys high with six windows on each floor. Cross the bridge. The eastern corner, where Union Street joins Union Terrace, provides an open space for the large granite and bronze group of statuary by Alfred Drury (1914), depicting Edward VII and the triumphs of peace. On the opposite corner is the Northern Assurance building which was designed by A. Marshall Mackenzie in 1885. It follows the style of other buildings in the street with its semicircular pillared portico.

When Union Street was constructed the plan for the city was to redevelop the housing in a series of squares from this end of Union Street to as far as Skene Street on the north and Alford Place on the west. It was never completed, but turn along South

Silver Street to Golden Square where the granite ashlar houses of simple but fine design show the beginning of the plan. No 13 is thought to be by Archibald Simpson. In the middle of the central garden is a granite statue by Thomas Campbell (1842) of George, fifth and last Duke of Gordon. The houses in the square are now all offices and the central area is usually packed with cars.

The south-west corner of Golden Square is the back of the Music Hall, usually considered to be one of Archibald Simpson's finest works. The foundation stone (at the corner of Union Street and South Silver Street) has this plaque: 'Aberdeen Public Rooms. Built by subscription, founded with Masonic honours by James Earl of Fife, Depute Grand Master of Scotland, April 26, 1820. First year of the reign of George the Fourth.' It is an interesting comment on the financing of civic buildings at this time that over £7000 was raised by public subscription for the Assembly Rooms. The committee under the Duke of Gordon also sponsored a competition to choose an architect for the scheme with 50 guineas, 30 guineas and 10 guineas for the first, second and third prizes.

Archibald Simpson was the prize-winner and his own description serves to depict the complex very well. 'The end front of it is in Union Street and . . . extends to 90 feet. It is decorated with a portico of six columns of the Greek Ionic order, being 30 feet in height and projecting 10 feet from the wall. The building has Silver Street on the east, along which it extends 156 feet.

The principal entrance under the portico

conducts into an outer vestibule having a flight of six steps leading to the Grand Salon, which is 68 feet in length by 20 feet wide and is divided into three compartments by fluted Ionic columns with ornamental capitals and corresponding pilasters. The centre part is 32 feet high and the ceiling is a dome finished with coppering.

In the centre of the building, and opening into the Salon through a screen of columns is a spacious gallery or promenade 70 feet in length, furnished with pilasters and an arched and panelled ceiling. It accommodates, on one side, the Ballroom, which is 70 feet long, 25 feet broad and 35 feet high, with segmentally arched ceiling, and on the other side the Supper or Refreshment Room (now the Square Room) which is a rotunda. It is decorated with eight fluted Corinthian columns and corresponding pilasters, over which the entablature forms a circle of 34 feet in diameter, from which springs the ceiling in the form of a flat dome with eight compartments intended to be filled with appropriate paintings. Within the columns are four spacious recesses for sofas, with niches in the wall.'

The concert room, called the Music Hall, which now gives its name to the whole complex, was added in 1859 by James Matthews, one of Simpson's pupils. The rooms continue to cater for a wide range of the citizens' activities from jumble sales to symphony concerts.

On the opposite side of Union Street to South Silver Street, Crown Street stretches southwards. Look down it at the impressive example of 'Balmorality', the castellated General Post Office designed by James Cumming Wynnes and completed in 1906. Walk up Union Street on this side and take the next street on the left, Dee Street. This joins Langstane Place a short way along, and here you can see, embedded in the wall, a surviving monolith from a nearby stone circle.

The land in this western part of Union Street and its surrounds originally belonged to the Seven Incorporated Trades of the city. They paid for the development of various streets, for example the Hammer Men paid for Crown Street, Golden Square and Silver Street, and the Tailors Bon Accord Street and Bon Accord Crescent. Walk down Bon Accord Street. (Bon Accord is the city's motto.) Telephone House was designed in 1908 by Leonard Stokes, a London architect. Turn along the short East Craibstone Street into Bon Accord Square.

In the centre garden a granite monolith commemorates 'Archibald Simpson, Architect 1790-1847. A pioneer of civic design in his native city'. The number of times his name is cited in this book bears witness to his prolific output. He studied at Marischal College and then in the office of James Massie, a local builder. In 1810 he went to London to the office of Robert Lugar, who published several books on the architecture of England and Scotland. Simpson then went to Italy and spent time in Rome and Florence before returning to Aberdeen in 1813. The building boom in the city gave him the opportunity to design a wide range of public and private buildings, both in his own city and more widely in the north-east. His slightly older contemporary, John Smith, became City Architect of Aberdeen, and the two men determined a style in the city which preserves its character to the present day.

Archibald Simpson designed Bon Accord Square and Crescent. In the former the houses are built in light-grey granite ashlar, two storeys high with basements and attics. The Crescent overlooks the south-west of the city which drops away beneath it. The end houses, Nos 1 and 2, 18 and 19 are straight, while Nos 3-17 are curved.

Walk back to Union Street, noticing on the west corner with Bon Accord Street, James Matthews' Langstane Church of 1868-69. The building is in Gothic style in freestone, with a 175-foot spire. The church stands back from the main line of the street. Cross Union Street again to the Music Hall. The building which stands next to it, the modern YMCA, is an unattractive replacement of an earlier John Smith structure. In the next street on the right, Huntly Street, is St Mary's Catholic Cathedral. It was built in 1859-60 by Alexander Ellis and the spire was added by his partner, R. G. Wilson, in 1877. The cathedral has a nave and aisles with a clerestory above. The statue of St Mary was sculpted by the Aberdonian Alexander Brodie. Back in Union Street, at the corner of Union Street and Summer Street, there is another Victorian Gothic church, Gilcomston South Church. It was designed in freestone by the architect of Balmoral, William Smith, and completed in 1868. Further up on the same side, beyond the turn to Rose Street, Nos 478-484 is a four-storey building by the city architect John Smith. It has square pillars projecting from the wall between the first and third storeys. The building was originally designed as the Union Street Cistern for the city's water supply, but is now offices.

Crossing Union Street once again there is St James' Episcopal Church, a granite Gothic structure built in 1887. To finish the walk cross the road at Holburn Junction and go along Alford Place. Christ's College has buildings on both sides of the road. The library and chapel are on the right-hand side of the road, and the Presbytery contains a portrait of William Robertson Smith, who held a Chair of Hebrew at Christ's College (1870-1881). He was tried for heresy and dismissed from his chair because of articles he wrote in the *Encyclopaedia Britannica,* incorporating new criticism of biblical sources. He later became Professor of Arabic in Cambridge.

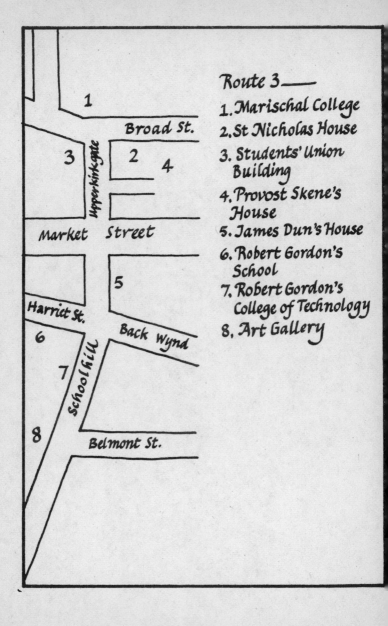

Route 3 ——
1. Marischal College
2. St Nicholas House
3. Students' Union Building
4. Provost Skene's House
5. James Dun's House
6. Robert Gordon's School
7. Robert Gordon's College of Technology
8. Art Gallery

Broad St.

Upperkirkgate

Market Street

Harriet St.

Back Wynd

Schoolhill

Belmont St.

Route 3

MARISCHAL COLLEGE TO THE ART GALLERY

THIS WALK IS GOOD FOR A WET AFTERNOON because the distance covered is short and most of the buildings mentioned can be visited. Begin in Broad Street at Marischal College, now one of the constituent colleges of Aberdeen University. It was originally founded as a university in its own right in April 1593 by the Protestant, George, fifth Earl Marischal, to rival King's College (see Route 8). The two colleges were united by Act of Parliament in 1860, Arts and Divinity being housed at King's, and the Natural Sciences, Medicine and Law at Marischal. Now with most faculties on the Old Aberdeen site and the Medical School at Foresterhill, Marischal College contains only Geology and Engineering, but its large public rooms are used for degree-giving and other formal university functions. The quadrangle, with its windows suitably boarded up, is the scene of the traditional fight by the students in their campaign to choose a Rector for the university. Aberdeen retains the medieval method of choosing the Rector who represents their interests by the votes of the 'nations', Mar, Buchan, Moray and Angus.

The perpendicular Gothic facade of the building, a style now enjoying a revival of interest in the Betjeman era, was the work of the architect, A. Marshall Mackenzie, and was completed in 1906. (An old news reel film still in existence of the opening by King Edward VII and Queen Alexandra, shows the old tenement houses of the Gallowgate which have now been pulled down to make room for modern developments.)

The buildings, in a more restrained Victorian Gothic, on the inner three sides of the quadrangle were the work of Archibald Simpson in the 1830s and 40s. They replaced the old Marischal College which in its turn had destroyed the old buildings of the medieval Greyfriars' monastery which stood on the site. On the far (east) side, opposite the gateway, is the Mitchell Tower, 235 feet high and one of the landmarks in Aberdeen. Its name and that of the graduation hall derive from the benefactions of Charles Mitchell and his son. As you enter the doorway at this end you are faced with the defiant motto of the Earls Marischal: 'They haif said; quhat say they; let thame say'.

Upstairs is the Picture Gallery where there is a historically-interesting collection of University portraits. (The University's finest pictures, including a portrait of its founder, Bishop Elphinstone, and early views of King's College are hung in rooms in King's College, Old Aberdeen, unseen even by most members of the University.)

It is well worth looking at the Anthropological Museum, also on the upper floor. The core of the collection is made up of objects donated by former

students of the University. In 1805 Robert Wilson of
Glenairnie Cottage, near Forres, went out as Ship's
Surgeon to the East India Company and sub-
sequently visited Egypt, Palestine and Persia. On
his death in 1871 he left his library and 'curiosities'
to Marischal College. Another benefactor was
Alexander Thomson (1798-1868) of Banchory
House who left a vast conglomeration of ancient
Egyptian and African objects. There are also
Nepalese figures, a wide variety of musical
instruments from all over the world, as well as
Greek and Roman statuary. The stuffed tiger,
unfortunately, has been put away. Apart from the
interest of individual items, the collection is a
fascinating commentary on gentlemanly tastes in
the late 18th and 19th centuries.

Come out of Marischal College and cross the road
to the Upperkirkgate, noticing on the left St
Nicholas House, monument to the growth of
Aberdeen city bureaucracy, and on the right-hand
corner, the Students' Union Building, shabby but
full of nostalgia for those who have studied at
Aberdeen University. Turn left along Guest Row,
and in the shadow of the high modern buildings
you will see Provost Skene's House. Now part of
Aberdeen Art Gallery and Museum, its restoration
was begun in 1951. The house is a fine example of
an early modern merchant's house. In form like the
medieval tower house, the building is constructed
of granite rubble with dressed stonework round the
doors and windows. The coat of arms of Sir George
Skene is over the main doorway and his motto:
'Gratis a Deo data' (Thanks be to God). The thistle

and rose motifs commemorate the restoration of Charles II in 1660.

Sir George Skene (1619-1707), Provost of Aberdeen, who gave his name to the house, added the corner turret stairs, replaced the pitched roof with a flat one and introduced more windows. The finest room in the house, called the Chapel, is a painted gallery with a series of tempera paintings on wood. There are ten rectangular panels linked by a pattern of sacred decorative emblems, such as the Five Sacred Wounds and the Cock symbolising Peter's denial of Christ. The paintings represent the life of Christ and the Coronation of Mary as Queen of Heaven. Only five pictures survive, but the Annunciation and the Resurrection are particularly fine. The kitchen in the basement has been turned into a coffee-room, and the other rooms in the house have been furnished to illustrate various periods, such as a Georgian dining-room and a 17th-century bedroom.

Return to the Upperkirkgate, walk down the hill, cross the traffic lights and walk up the other side. The street is now called Schoolhill. At the top of the incline on the left is James Dun's House, No 61 Schoolhill. This is a very attractive small 18th-century house of hand-dressed granite ashlar with door and window jambs in darker stone. The architect is not known, but it is possible that it was William Law who designed the Bannerman Bridge in Marischal Street. James Dun (c 1708-1789), the son of a prosperous city merchant, became Rector of the Grammar School in 1744. (Schoolhill takes its name from this school although the institution has now moved.) The house was restored in the 1970s and taken over in 1975 as the children's section of the Museum. It has an attractive permanent collection of toys and objects of social and domestic history, while the ground floor often displays special exhibitions.

Across the road, standing back with a tree-lined lawn in front, is the arched entrance to Robert Gordon's School and Robert Gordon's College of Technology. The original building, the central block as you look through the gateway, is the work of William Adam, father of Robert, and was finished in 1739. Robert Gordon was an Aberdeen Merchant who traded with the Baltic and he founded the college as a pious foundation for the education of the sons of impoverished burgesses in the city. It is now a public boarding and day school. The statue outside is of General Gordon of Khartoum (no relation to the other Gordon) and is by T. Stuart Burnett. It is cast in bronze and dates from 1888.

Next door to Robert Gordon's on the same side of Schoolhill is the Art Gallery, built by public subscription and opened in 1885. Originally the building housed an art school and a gallery, but Gray's School of Art was moved to Garthdee. The building is of pink granite in Renaissance style by A. Marshall Mackenzie. The war memorial and lion on the corner, and the Cowdray Hall behind them were added in 1925.

The Art Gallery contains a fine collection of paintings and sculpture. It has works by important European painters, such as Pisarro's *Effet de neige à l'Hermitage, Pontoise, 1879*, but it is particularly strong on British Art. A selection must necessarily be subjective, but look at Paul Nash's *Wood on the Downs*, and the small *Seated Girl holding a piece of Sewing* by Gwen John. The Scottish School is represented through all its range from the Aberdonian George Jamesone's self portrait to works by modern painters such as Joan Eardley and Anne Redpath. The funds of the MacDonald Bequest ensure that modern works can be bought. Upstairs look at the James McBey Print Room which houses a magnificent collection of this (underrated) Aberdeenshire artist's work, including drawings he did as a War Artist in World War I and also topographical studies (see Route 15). There is a small but good selection of sculptures downstairs, particularly Barbara Hepworth's *Oval Form—Trezion*. Look too at the Scottish Silver which is on display.

The tour of the Art Gallery ends the walk.

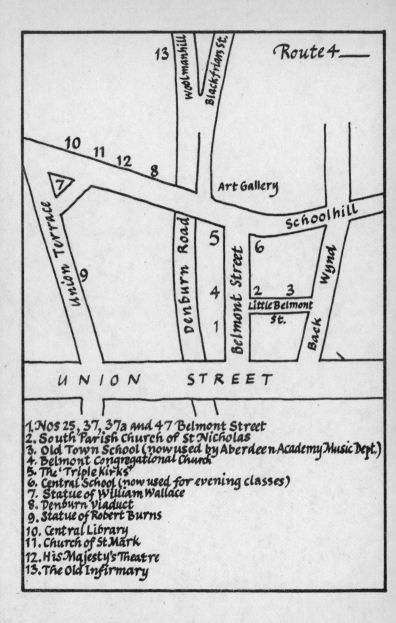

1. Nos 25, 37, 37a and 47 Belmont Street
2. South Parish Church of St Nicholas
3. Old Town School (now used by Aberdeen Academy Music Dept.)
4. Belmont Congregational Church
5. The 'Triple Kirks'
6. Central School (now used for evening classes)
7. Statue of William Wallace
8. Denburn Viaduct
9. Statue of Robert Burns
10. Central Library
11. Church of St Mark
12. His Majesty's Theatre
13. The Old Infirmary

Route 4

BELMONT STREET TO WOOLMANHILL

BEGIN THIS WALK AT JUST BELOW UNION Terrace. The narrowness of the street after the width of Union Street gives an impression of what pre-19th-century Aberdeen must have been like. Belmont Street and Little Belmont Street, which leaves it at right angles about halfway down on the east side, were constructed in the 1780s and there are still some town houses of that period to be seen. Nos 25, 37, 37a and 47 Belmont Street are worth looking at. If you can get into the courtyard of No 25, there is a coat of arms of an early Provost of Aberdeen, Thomas Menzies of Pitfodels (1525), and another of the Irvines of Drum whom we have already seen in St Nicholas Kirk.

On the right-hand side as you walk down, at the corner of Little Belmont Street is the South Parish Church of St Nicholas. John Smith designed it in 1830-31. It is on a T-plan with a tower at the front in perpendicular style. The material is granite ashlar with wood tracery. It is no longer used as a church but as social meeting-rooms for the Church of Scotland (called Kirk House).

Walk along Little Belmont Street. Ahead of you in

the distance is St Nicholas Kirk. You get a fine view of the East Church and the steeple from here. On the north side of the street is a small classical building, designed by John Smith in 1841. It is a granite single-storey E-plan design with a tetrastyle unfluted Doric colonnade between wings, and with a pediment above. It was built as the old Town School, and later taken over by Aberdeen Academy. It is now used by the Music Departments of schools in Aberdeen.

Turn back to Belmont Street. On the western side is the Belmont Congregational Church. It is in Italian Romanesque style with an apse at the east end. Further along the road on the same side are the 'Triple Kirks'. They were built in 1844 at the Disruption, the split in the church caused by lay interference in church affairs, to take members who had left the St Nicholas congregation, the three churches representing divisions among the protesters. The architect is once again Archibald Simpson, and he chose an early pointed Gothic style, rubble-built with brick dressings, and a tall brick spire copied from Marburg Cathedral. The churches were allowed to fall into disrepair in the 1960s and 70s, but they have now been sold for commercial purposes although the spire is to be preserved. The east church, Belmont Church, is now Simpson's Restaurant, at least some recognition of a distinguished architect.

On the east corner of Belmont Street and Schoolhill is a building designed in 1901 by J. Ogg Allen for the Aberdeen School Board who opened it as the Central School. It later became the

Aberdeen Academy. (The school has now moved to Hazlehead, and the building is used by the Education Department for evening classes and other activities.) The structure is a Renaissance-style building with a leaded dome at the corner. There are Doric columns at the windows below. The top storey has Venetian-style windows.

Turn to the left along Schoolhill. (Opposite is the Art Gallery and the War Memorial. See Route 3). Over the Rosemount Viaduct you come to Union Terrace Gardens on the left. On an island site at the end of Union Terrace is an imposing statue of William Wallace cast in bronze by W. Grant Stevenson in 1888. A great sword is held in his outstretched right hand and the inscription records his life's achievments.

The 1883 Aberdeen Extension and Improvements Act ordered the building of viaducts over the Denburn at the north end. William Boulton was the engineer for the granite Rosemount Viaduct and the Denburn Viaduct on the other side of Schoolhill.

Before crossing to look at this side look along Union Terrace which contains a row of late-19th-century buildings including the massive Caledonian Hotel. No 22 Union Terrace was designed by A. Marshall Mackenzie in Renaissance style. No 16 is the only 18th-century house in the row. Across the road above the Gardens is Henry Bain Smith's bronze statue of Robert Burns with the daisy he called the 'wee, modest, crimson-tipped flow'r' in his hand.

Return to Schoolhill and cross the road to see

three buildings, known to Aberdonians as 'Education, Salvation and Damnation'. First is the Central Library, built in 1892 and rebuilt inside in 1981. Next door is the Church of St Mark designed by the architect A. Marshall Mackenzie and completed in the same year as the library. It has a dome and a granite portico with Corinthian columns. Next door to that again is His Majesty's Theatre. Its architect Frank Matcham built it in pink granite and faced it with white Kemnay granite. It was opened in 1906. The theatre has been used for visiting theatrical companies, for Scottish Opera, for Scottish Ballet and for annual pantomimes. It is at present (1981) closed for complete reconstruction, when, sadly in some ways, the large auditorium will be divided into two theatres; but the prospect of a resident repertory company in the smaller auditorium banishes sentimentality.

Cross over the Denburn Viaduct where you see plainly the magnificence of the engineering feat in spanning this valley. Walk along towards the Art Gallery, then turn left down Woolmanhill. The walk ends at the Old Infirmary, a fine granite ashlar building, designed by Archibald Simpson. It has an egg-shaped dome which appears at the apex of the porticos on each face. The work was completed in the years 1832-9.

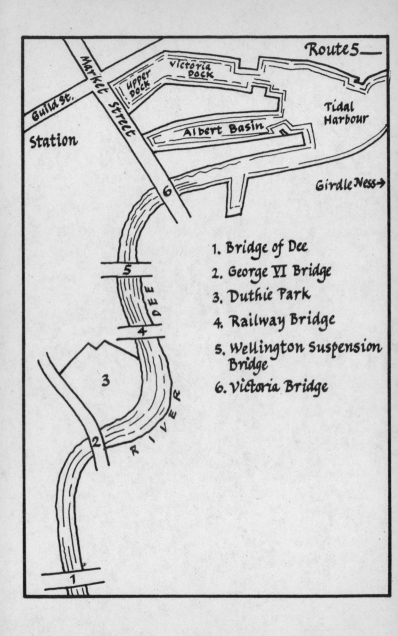

Route 5

BRIDGE OF DEE TO GIRDLENESS

TAKE A NO 1, 2 OR 3 BUS FROM UNION STREET to Bridge of Dee and get off on the north bank of the river. The Bridge of Dee was built originally in the first quarter of the 16th century, but it was widened in 1841-2 by the engineer John Smith. It is now a seven-span bridge of dressed stone with segmented anchor and cutwaters extended upwards to make semi-hexagonal pedestrian refuges. This bridge replaced the Ruthrieston Pack Horse Bridge built in 1693, which still survives further eastwards along Riverside Drive between the motorway and the river. Continue along Riverside Drive eastwards to the George VI Bridge built in 1939 by the engineer Sir Frank Mears. It is a four-span reinforced concrete bridge with three main elliptical arches, and a flood arch faced with granite.

Leave Riverside Drive and go into Duthie Park. In the spring the steep banks facing the river are covered with thousands of bulbs, and it is in this park that the City's Links and Parks Department have their trial grounds for the plants which enrich the city and have won for it the title 'City in Bloom' on eight occasions since 1965.

Duthie Park was gifted to the city by Miss Elizabeth Crombie Duthie who bought up land in the area, including the estate of Arthurseat which had to be acquired by Act of Parliament. A statue of Hygeia, the goddess of good health, with four lions at its base commemorates the gift and also the opening ceremony by HRH Princess Beatrice on September 27 1883.

On the southern side of the park stands a large obelisk which used to be in the quadrangle of Marischal College. It was erected in memory of Sir James McGrigor, Bart, MD, KCB etc, of the Army Medical Department and Rector of Marischal College. Born in Strathspey in 1771, he served abroad in numerous places including 'the deserts of Thebes and Suez'. The Duke of Wellington said 'I consider him one of the most industrious, able and successful public servants I have ever met with'. The inscription ends 'In the course of fifty-seven years of active service he was exposed to the vicissitudes of war and climate besides encountering shipwreck and other dangers at sea: yet he lived to attain a tranquil and happy old age'. He died in London in April 1858.

Walk on from here in a clockwise direction. On the west side of the park are several small ornamental lakes with swans and ducks. There is a large mound near the Great Southern Road gate which used to be the wilderness end of the park, but now sadly it has been domesticated with ranks of rose bushes and a garden seat. An attractive bandstand dominates the central grassy area. The northern side has peacocks and deer in cages and a magnificent Winter Garden. In a terrible act of vandalism the old Victorian conservatory was taken down in the sixties, but the new greenhouses have been splendidly planned. The largest house has pools full of fish, and temperate shrubs like hibiscus and weigelia flourish. Some of the plants have attractive histories. One camellia was planted from a cutting of a shrub planted by Lady James Hay in the conservatory of Seaton House in 1865.

Return to Riverside Drive and continue towards the mouth of the Dee. The noise of traffic on this stretch of the walk makes it less than attractive, but it is worth persisting to see the curve of the river and the lower bridges. The railway reached Aberdeen in 1850 and the next bridge takes it across the river. Further down is the Wellington Suspension Bridge, built in 1829-31 by two architects: John Smith for the masonry and Samuel Brown for the ironwork. The wooden deck is steel-framed now. Originally the frame and the rods from which the chains are suspended were made of iron. Flat-link chains support the bridge. The lowest bridge is the Victoria Bridge built in 1881 by the engineer V. H. Blyth. It is a five-span dressed-stone bridge with segmented arches and a polished granite parapet.

You are now at the Harbour. From here you can walk along Crombie Road, Abbey Road and Girdleness Road to the lighthouse, or take a No 10 bus through Torry to the same point. Girdleness Lighthouse was built in 1833 by the engineer Robert Stevenson. It is a tapering tower with two lanterns, only the top one of which is used. The keepers' houses are single-storey with flat roofs.

The view of the harbour from the south side is probably the best view you can get. Opposite is the north pier, built originally from a plan by John Smeaton from 1769-80. The pier was extended 900 feet by Telford in 1810-16 and finally extended by 500 feet in 1874. On the south side is the South Breakwater built in 1868.

The Dee forms the first ingress. The next is the Albert Basin developed in 1879 by Act of Parliament. On its north side a new Fish Market was competed in 1889. It is still worthwhile making an early-morning expedition to a Fish Sale, although the decline of the industry means that it is not the dramatic event it was a few years ago. You need to get there by 6.00 am at least, and even then proceedings will be well under way. The third branch of the harbour contains the Upper Dock and the Victoria Dock, formerly separated by the Regent Hydraulic Bridge. Both these docks were originally enclosed, but since 1972 they have been converted to tidal working. The harbour area has been fenced off in the past few years so you can no longer get the impression of ships at the end of the street.

Walk back along Guild Street to the Station.

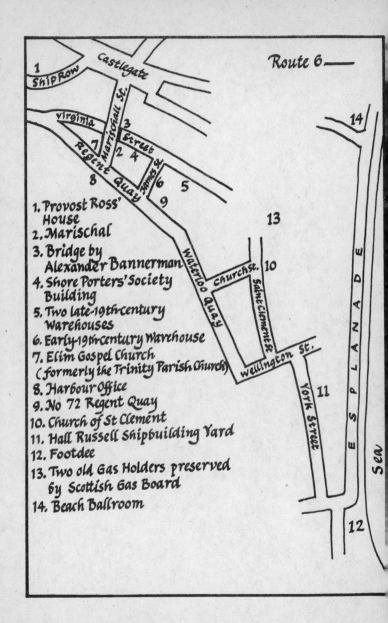

Route 6

1. Provost Ross' House
2. Marischal
3. Bridge by Alexander Bannerman
4. Shore Porters' Society Building
5. Two late-19th-century Warehouses
6. Early-19th-century Warehouse
7. Elim Gospel Church (formerly the Trinity Parish Church)
8. Harbour Office
9. No 72 Regent Quay
10. Church of St Clement
11. Hall Russell Shipbuilding Yard
12. Footdee
13. Two old Gas Holders preserved by Scottish Gas Board
14. Beach Ballroom

SHIPROW TO FOOTDEE AND THE BEACH

THIS WALK BRINGS YOU INTO CONTACT WITH
Aberdeen's maritime past and present. Begin by
the Union Buildings at the foot of Union Street and
walk along to the end of the block. Here you will
see an opening on your left. This is Shiprow. Much
of it was pulled down to make a modern super-
market and multi-storey car park. The one
remaining building of note is on the right-hand side
(west) as you walk down the hill. The house, known
as Provost Ross' House after one of its owners,
dates from 1593. It is a rectangular building with
gabled towers, projecting at the front and back.
The two next-door houses, Nos 48 and 50 (1710),
have also been preserved. Provost Ross' House, for
a long time the home of the British Council in
Aberdeen, has now been designated to house the
City's Maritime Museum, at present existing
uncomfortably in basement rooms by the Cowdray
Hall next to the Art Gallery.

Retrace your steps to the Castlegate and take the
next road to the east and walk down towards the
harbour. This is Marischal Street and is the only
remaining street of Georgian buildings in the city.

The street was built three years after the purchase and pulling down of the old Marischal's Lodging by the Town Council in 1763. The 40-feet-wide street was paved with granite setts, later to become popular in other parts of the town. The houses are three-storeyed with attics and three windows to each frontage. Variety comes in the addition of pillars as at No 46, or by decorative fanlights as at No 48.

In order to cross Virginia Street, a single-arch bridge was built in 1766-7 by Alexander Bannerman to the design of William Law, the first attempt to try to span the levels of Aberdeen. The bridge was replaced in 1973 to accommodate the ring road beneath.

The view from the bridge is of Virginia Street below. Looking down on the left, you can see the Shore Porters' Society Building, on the corner of Virginia Street and Shore Lane. It was built in 1897, and is a granite ashlar building of five storeys with seven by six bays. At the corner is a corbelled turret with the date inscribed. The Shore Porters' 'removal' vans which can be seen in the city and throughout the country proclaim that they were founded in 1498. This is the date of the earliest entry in the Town Council Register which mentions the 'pynours', or porters, who worked on the quayside. Organised into a guild, they may have been in existence even before this. They have continued to be a society, governed by their own rules revised in 1896 from the accumulated regulations of centuries. After twenty-one years' service each member is entitled to receive benefits from their funds, and each member is a shareholder in the business.

Virginia Street, accessible from the quay at the bottom of the brae, also has two other late-19th-century warehouses, one a three-storeyed building with seven bays and four chimneys, and another rubble-built with four storeys and attic, five arched cart entries, dormer windows and a central hoist. James Street, off the quay, contains an early-19th-century warehouse of three storeys with attic and basement. There are six bays of rubble building with two hoists and a central elliptically-arched cart entry. The names of the streets round the harbour, such as Virginia Street, Baltic Street and Cotton Street, give some indications of the areas and products with which Aberdeen has been connected at various periods of her trading history.

But to return to Marischal Street continue from the bridge to the harbour. At the bottom on the right is the Elim Gospel Church, a granite building in Gothic style which was formerly the Trinity Parish Church, although it was built originally in 1788-94 as the Theatre Royal. It remained a theatre until 1872 and the alley behind it is still called Theatre Lane. The theatre dressing-rooms are now a workshop.

The quays which turn to right and left at the bottom of Marischal Street are successively, from the roundabout at the bottom of Market Street, Trinity Quay, Regent Quay and Waterloo Quay. All harbour constructions south of these quays are discussed in Route 5. Nos 14-16 Regent Quay houses the Harbour Office. Built in 1883-5 by A.

Marshall Mackenzie, four storeys high, the building has eight bays with round-headed openings on the ground floor and a pediment. The clock tower has a domed roof. No 35 is the old Customs House, originally built in Renaissance style by James Gordon of Cobairdy in 1771. The three-storied building, of granite ashlar, has very fine windows and a pedimented door approached by a flight of four steps. No 72 Regent Quay is an old sugar refinery dating from the late 18th to the early 19th century. The complex contains a seven-storey rubble building, a five-storey and two-attic store with a gabled front and a two-storey office.

Continue along Waterloo Quay and turn to the left at Church Street. Opposite at the end is the Church of St Clement. A chapel was erected to the saint in 1498. A new church was built in 1631 and in 1788 the present building was begun and added to in the 19th century.

Turn right along St Clement Street until you reach York Place, and then turn right along York Street. This part of town belongs to the shipbuilding firm of Hall Russell, the successors of A. Hall and Co who built the Aberdeen clippers including the *Thermopylae*, which won the title of fastest clipper in the world after beating her rival the *Cutty Sark*, built on the Clyde. Hall Russell continue to build a variety of ships, such as trawlers, tugs and ferries, although demand for the first is declining rapidly. At the end of this road on the right is the Pocra Quay now used by North Sea Oil supply ships.

Turn up to the left and you arrive at Footdee, pronounced either 'Fittie' or 'Futty'. This village was commissioned by the Town Council in the early 19th century as a model village to replace the shacks of the fisher families. The city architect, John Smith, designed it in 1808-10, building single-storey but-and-ben cottages round two squares, North Square and South Square. Pilot's Square was added later. The elder Smith designed four more houses in 1837, and his son William Smith, added the Footdee Mission Hall in 1869, and built houses in Pilot's Square in 1873. After 1880 when the council allowed owners to buy their houses, individual additions were made to some buildings. Nearly a century later in 1970, the Council drew up a plan for restoring the village and provided grants for doing so, and it is now a conservation area. You can take a No 14 bus from here to the Castlegate.

If you feel like walking farther, follow the Esplanade north with the Queen's Links on the left. The industrial archaeology enthusiast will admire the two old gas holders preserved by the Scottish Gas Board. The horizontal steam engines and original tools, also preserved in a nearby building, need a special visit. Further along the Esplanade is the Beach Ballroom with its Northern Lights Room and restaurants. Two miles of beach stretch from here to the Bridge of Don. Behind the beach are the Links, the city's golf-course since 1625. The Sea Beach proclaimed on the No 4 bus is rather a disappointment to those expecting the sea fronts of the south with their splendid hotels and cafés. Take the No 4 bus from the Beach Ballroom back to Union Street.

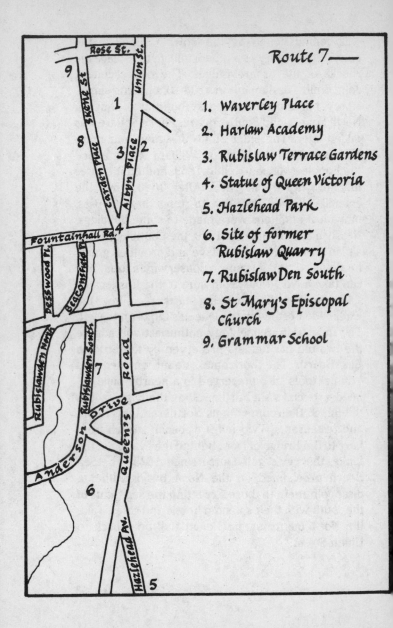

Route 7

1. Waverley Place
2. Harlaw Academy
3. Rubislaw Terrace Gardens
4. Statue of Queen Victoria
5. Hazlehead Park
6. Site of former
   Rubislaw Quarry
7. Rubislaw Den South
8. St Mary's Episcopal
   Church
9. Grammar School

THE WEST END

THIS ROUTE CAN BE EITHER A RATHER LONG 'street' walk, or it can be done partly on foot and partly by bus. It covers the Victorian middle-class development of the second part of the 19th century. The rows of substantial villas and terraces seem to sum up Aberdonian aspirations and prosperity.

Begin at Alford Place, by the south building of Christ's College, and either take a No 4 or 5 bus along Albyn Place, or walk in a westerly direction. The land of the first section was owned originally by James Skene of Rubislaw, a friend of Sir Walter Scott, and Waverley Place was named in honour of the novelist. Archibald Simpson was Skene's architect, and there are fine examples of his domestic building in the area: Nos 2-16 Albyn Place (c 1836), Nos 19 (c 1830), 21 (1830) and 28 (1838). Nos 26 and 29 are also possibly his designs. A public building by the same architect here, is the central building of Harlaw Academy, formerly the High School for Girls (1837-9). It was built originally as Mrs Elmslie's Institution for Orphan Girls. On the north side of Albyn Place the gardens of Rubislaw

Terrace lie in front of a row of houses commissioned by Skene from the architects Mackenzie and Matthews.

At the end of Albyn Place is an intersection where five roads meet. A bronze statue of Queen Victoria, bearing the inscription 'erected by the Royal Tradesmen of Aberdeen', stands in the middle of the road.

Queen's Cross Church at the junction of Albyn Place and Carden Place was designed by John Bridgeford Pirie. Follow Queen's Road and look at No 50, a curious, ornate villa by the same architect. It is perhaps worthwhile catching a bus along Queen's Road to Hazlehead Avenue which leads to Aberdeen's largest park, Hazlehead. The land was originally part of the Freedom Lands which Robert the Bruce granted the burgh in 1319. These lands were gradually alienated, and fell into private hands. In 1920 the city acquired 852 acres for a public park. Extensive woodlands as well as golf-courses and other facilities for recreation make it a popular place for the citizens. Some modern local-authority housing has been built in the park, with four 12-storey blocks and lower-level housing for the elderly.

Return along Queen's Road towards the city centre. On the northern side, at the junction with Royfold Crescent and Anderson Drive, is the site of the former Rubislaw Quarry, now partly filled in and used for building. The great building boom in 18th-century Aberdeen encouraged the opening of quarries at Dancing Cairns in 1750 and later at Ferryhill and Nigg. But the most important and best granite came from Rubislaw Quarry, which John Gibb, the superintendent of the harbour, acquired and began to exploit in the early 19th century. The blue-grey granite quarried here was distinctive and used for the finest work. William Diack writing on the *History of the Granite Industry in Aberdeen* noted that 'the rock of Rubislaw surpasses all other granites in Britain on account of the greater proportion of quartz it contains and its subsidiary minerals, besides quartz, felspar and mica, include albite, chalcedony, shorl and calcareous spar'. The quarry at its greatest extent was 900 feet long by 750 feet wide and 465 feet deep. In 1969 it was declared to be no longer economic to quarry granite here.

Turn a little way along Anderson Drive and you will come, on the east side, to Rubislaw Den South. This and Rubislaw Den North, are two of the most desirable residential streets in the city. Between them is a 'gorge' through which runs the Den Burn which eventually, after being channelled underground, reaches the harbour.

Cross Forest Road and walk back towards the city centre along Desswood Place or Beaconsfield Place, two of the 19th-century residential developments. Turn along Fountainhall Road towards Queen's Cross.

Take the left-hand fork at Queen's Cross along Carden Place and Skene Street. Alexander Ellis designed St Mary's Episcopal Church in Carden Place. It is known as the 'tartan kirk' because of its multi-coloured stonework. Albert Street and Victoria Street, which lead off Carden Place and

Skene Street, have terraces of attractive houses, now mostly offices.

On the north side of Skene Street is the Grammar School, a granite ashlar building with turrets and crow-stepped gables, built in 1863. A statue of Lord Byron, who was once a pupil at the school, by Pittendrigh McGillivray, stands in front of the building.

Walk back along Rose Street to Union Street.

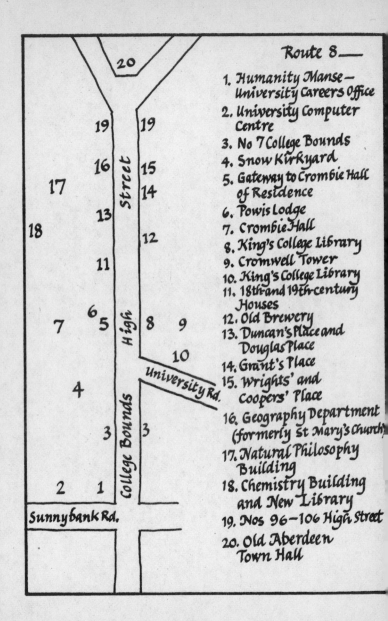

Route 8 —

1. Humanity Manse — University Careers Office
2. University Computer Centre
3. No 7 College Bounds
4. Snow Kirkyard
5. Gateway to Crombie Hall of Residence
6. Powis Lodge
7. Crombie Hall
8. King's College Library
9. Cromwell Tower
10. King's College Library
11. 18th and 19th-century Houses
12. Old Brewery
13. Duncan's Place and Douglas Place
14. Grant's Place
15. Wrights' and Coopers' Place
16. Geography Department (formerly St Mary's Church)
17. Natural Philosophy Building
18. Chemistry Building and New Library
19. Nos 96–106 High Street
20. Old Aberdeen Town Hall

OLD ABERDEEN: KING'S COLLEGE

TAKE THE NO 20 BUS FROM LITTLEJOHN
Street at the side of Marischal College. It sweeps
down to the new regional road, round the huge
Mounthooly roundabout, covered in daffodils in the
spring and then worth a visit in its own right. The
bus then joins the old north-east road to Old
Aberdeen, along Mounthooly where you notice on
the left two streets, Canal Street and Jute Street,
reminders in name only of an earlier industrial age.
On the corner of Canal Street new council housing,
awarded a Civic Design Award, has replaced older
houses. The bus continues along the Spital named
after a medieval charitable foundation which stood
on the right on the brow of the hill where the new
housing development, St Peter's Court, perpetuates
its name.

Get off the bus at Sunnybank Road and walk
down towards College Bounds. This is the begin-
ning of the University area. In December 1489 King
James IV granted a charter to William Elphinstone,
Bishop of Aberdeen, giving him the right to Old
Aberdeen 'as a bishop's seat and as a city for ever'.
Six years later the Bishop obtained a papal bull

from Alexander IV, the Borgia Pope, to found a *Studium Generale,* or University with all faculties. This became King's College. The Bishop's aim was to provide higher education for those people in the north-east of Scotland who had no opportunity because of the difficulties of travel to reach other places of learning. He hoped that 'By earnest study' the student might 'win the pearl of knowledge, which shows the way to living well and happily, by its value makes the learned far to surpass the unlearned, leads to a clear understanding of the secrets of the universe, helps the untaught and raises to eminence those born in the lowest estate'.

On the left, as you walk down the hill you pass Humanity Manse, once the residence of the professors of Latin, but now the Careers Office of the University. Above on the hill is the University Computer Centre (entrance in Sunnybank Road). The terraced houses in College Bounds, the name of this stretch of the road, are mostly 19th-century, two-storey granite ashlar houses, although No 7 is of the previous century. Inside the entrance to the student residence, Johnston Hall, on the left, is a path leading to the Snow Kirkyard, all that remains of the burgh church of Old Aberdeen, St Mary of the Snows. The legend of the dedication belongs to Rome and the miracle of the appearance of the Blessed Virgin and a fall of snow in summer in the city which led to the founding of Santa Maria Maggiore. The dedication was obviously more important in Aberdeen.

The two halls of residence, Johnston and Crombie, stand back on low ground; Crombie Hall on the marshland formed by the Powis Burn. The entrance to Crombie is through an ornate gateway with minarets, designed by architect Alexander Fraser in 1834 for John Leslie of Powis. To the right of this entrance stands Powis Lodge built in 1697. The house was extended in 1711, and its bow-fronted windows were added in 1829. They look out on the lawn in front of Crombie Hall, the first University residence opened in 1960.

Across the road stands King's College Chapel. The late Scottish Gothic building was begun in 1500 and finished some six years later during the lifetime of Bishop Elphinstone. Its most notable feature is the tower and crown, the only other crown in Scotland being the one on the High Kirk of St Giles in Edinburgh. The original one was destroyed in a storm in 1633, but was replaced a year later with additional ornamentation. The chapel was a collegiate church and inside it retains the screen which would have separated the canons from the rest of the congregation. The screen was moved to the west in 1870 to form an ante-chapel, now a War Memorial Chapel for the University. The east end is a three-sided apse. There is no nave and the chapel is dominated by the Flemish Gothic carved oak stalls. The oak ceiling is the work of John Fendour. Bishop William Stewart originally gave the carved pulpit, of unknown workmanship, to St Machar Cathedral, and it was removed to its present place in the last century.

The tombs of Bishop Elphinstone who died in 1514 and the first Principal of the University, Hector Boece, who died in 1536, are within the chapel. The cenotaph of Elphinstone outside the West Door is of a much later date and was cast in Venice just before World War I. On the north side of the exterior of the chapel are five consecration crosses, depicted as a circle in a cross. They mark the places at which the bishop would have anointed the chapel on its consecration. Twelve crosses were required inside the church, but these do not survive.

At the south-east corner of the chapel is the Cromwell Tower, built in 1658, originally as lodgings, but now used as lecture rooms. Further to the east in the quadrangle is King's College Library (1885), a long hall with double transepts and a vaulted ceiling, spoilt by the post-war split-level flooring put in to house more books. The library contains many treasures, including a medieval Bestiary and an illuminated Hebrew Codex of the Bible copied at the end of the 15th century by Jewish refugees from Spain. The MacBean Room, also in the quadrangle, contains a collection of material on the local history of the region.

Return to the road which now changes its name from College Bounds to High Street. The buildings here and in the Chanonry, and in Don and Dunbar Streets (see next route) form part of a conservation area. On the left (west) side the houses are late-18th- and early-19th-century two-storied houses in granite. On the right, the lawn beyond the chapel is surrounded by University buildings, Elphinstone Hall on the east, and New King's Building on the north, both 19th-century buildings. Next is the Old Brewery, restored for teaching rooms, but a reminder of the earlier activities of the old town. Several lanes lead from the High Street. Notice the pantiled houses in Duncan's Place and Douglas Place.

On the right in Grant's Place, the single-storied rubble cottages, originally built in 1732, were restored in the 1960s. Beyond them, Wrights' and Coopers' Place, also of the 18th century, were houses of skilled artisans. The row was restored by the MacRobert Trust. The sundial and the pond at the end have the inscription behind them: 'In memory of Lady MacRobert whose sons Alasdair, Roderic and Iain gave their lives 1938-1941. Per ardua ad astra'.

Opposite this row on the west side of the High Street is the former St Mary's Church, now part of the Geography Department. In front of it stands the Mercat Cross of Old Aberdeen with the insignia of the Virgin Mary, protector of the town, on its shaft. Behind the church and across the lawns to the left is the Natural Philosophy Building with its domed lecture hall and skilful mix of traditional granite with concrete and glass. Designed by a London architect, E. D. Jeffries Matthews, it is one of the most successful modern buildings in Aberdeen. Beyond it the Chemistry Building and the New Library, still in progress, are less elegant additions to the campus.

Return to the High Street. The houses further north were more prosperous dwellings. No 96 was built in 1623, No 108 in 1751, and Nos 100, 104 and 106 are all 18th-century.

Facing, on an island site at the end of the street, is

Old Aberdeen Town Hall. It has three storeys with three windows on each floor. The centre bay projects and has a clock stage and a cupola. It was built in 1721, but was altered in 1788 by the architect George Jaffrey. The arms of the burgh of Old Aberdeen are above the door. 'Azure, a bough pot or, changed with three salmon in fret proper, and containing three lilies of the garden, the dexter in bud, the centre in full bloom, the sinister half-blown, also proper, flowered argent.'

The walk ends here, so return to the city centre on a No 20 bus, or extend the walk by following Route 9.

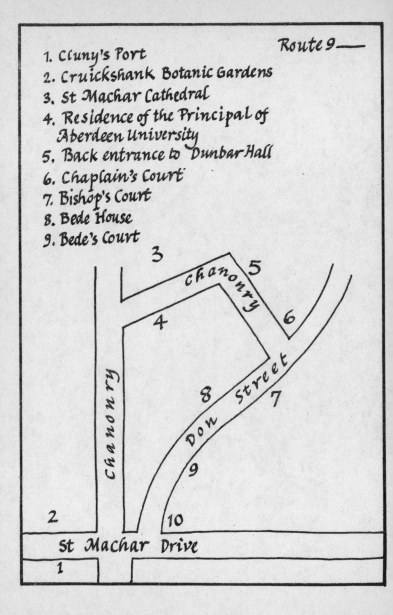

1. Cluny's Port
2. Cruickshank Botanic Gardens
3. St Machar Cathedral
4. Residence of the Principal of Aberdeen University
5. Back entrance to Dunbar Hall
6. Chaplain's Court
7. Bishop's Court
8. Bede House
9. Bede's Court

3

Chanonry

5

4

6

Chanonry

Don Street

8

7

9

2

10

St Machar Drive

1

Route 9

OLD ABERDEEN:
ST MACHAR CATHEDRAL AND THE CHANONRY

THIS WALK CONTINUES THE EXPLORATION OF Old Aberdeen. Cross St Machar Drive from the Town House. Just before you do so, notice to the left on St Machar Drive a small house called Cluny's Port. This would have been the site of one of the former gateways to the walled area which enclosed the Cathedral. Across the road to the left of the Chanonry are Cruickshank Botanic Gardens which belong to the University. They are laid out to show different types of planting. The newly-created rock and scree garden in the further part of the grounds is particularly worth seeing, but there are plants and trees in flower for most of the year. If you come out of the side gate you will find yourself in the Chanonry. Parts of the wall which originally divided the area from the rest of the town can still be seen.

The medieval Cathedral was served by a chapter of canons (French *Chanoine* which gave the name to the road), who lived within the enclave whose high walls and well-guarded gates were needed for protection. At the Reformation back in 1560 the canons' properties fell into lay hands and eventually became professional houses of the University. No 3 on the right is a 1930s building which fits in discreetly with the 18th- and 19th-century houses in the rest of the Chanonry. No 9 on the left, before you turn towards the Cathedral, is an alms house, Mitchell's Hospital, an H-plan group of single-storied rubble houses with a centre gable surmounted by a bell-tower. The courtyard in front has a sundial. The benefactor endowed the houses in 1801 to support five widows and five unmarried daughters of 'merchant and trade burgesses of Old Aberdeen'.

Across the road is the entrance to St Machar Cathedral. Legend has it that St Machar, who was sent forth on a mission by St Columba, was told to found a church where he saw a bend of a river that formed a shepherd's crook. The Don does so at this point, and the foundation was made in 580AD. The see of Aberdeen was not established until 1158. Only a few stones of the Norman church survive. The Cathedral was rebuilt after the devastations of Edward III's army in 1336 and the nave was completed between 1424 and 1440. The granite ashlar facing is the first use of dressed granite in Aberdeen. The west end has two embattled towers, with freestone spires which were added during the episcopacy of Gavin Dunbar (1518-1532). The west window is divided by six mullions into seven openings in the perpendicular style. A Charter Room over the south porch contains Cathedral service books of the 15th and 16th centuries as well as later Kirk Session records.

Bishop Dunbar's greatest gift to the Cathedral in 1520 was the panelled-oak heraldic ceiling. The forty-eight shields commemorate royal, ecclesiastical names.

North Side
1. The Holy Roman Emperor (Charles V)
2. The King of France
3. The King of Spain
4. The King of England
5. The King of Denmark
6. The King of Hungary
7. The King of Portugal
8. The King of Aragon
9. The King of Cyprus
10. The King of Navarre
11. The King of Sicily
12. The King of Poland
13. The King of Bohemia
14. The Duke of Bourbon
15. The Duke of Guelders
16. Old Aberdeen

Middle Row
1. Pope Leo X
2. Archbishop of St Andrews
3. Archbishop of Glasgow
4. Bishop of Dunkeld
5. Bishop of Aberdeen
6. Bishop of Moray
7. Bishop of Ross
8. Bishop of Brechin
9. Bishop of Caithness

10. Bishop of Galloway
11. Bishop of Dunblane
12. Bishop of Lismore
13. Bishop of Orkney
14. Bishop of Isles
15. Prior of St Andrews
16. University of Aberdeen

South Side
1. The King of Scots (James V)
2. St Margaret
3. Duke of Albany
4. The Earl of March
5. The Earl of Moray
6. The Earl of Douglas
7. The Earl of Angus
8. The Earl of Mar
9. The Earl of Sutherland
10. The Earl of Crawford
11. The Earl of Huntly
12. The Earl of Argyll
13. The Earl of Errol
14. The Earl Marischal
15. The Earl of Bothwell
16. New Aberdeen

Bishop Elphinstone (1483-1514), the founder of the University, had begun a new choir for the Cathedral, but it was never completed, and the building was screened at the east side of the crossing. The central tower fell in 1688 and was never replaced. The building was neglected in the 16th and 17th centuries and suffered under

Cromwell, Its glass is 19th-century. In the south aisle on the east wall of the tower a monument to Bishop Scougall (1664-82) remains. There is one medieval monument on the south wall of the south aisle to Simon Dodis, a canon of Aberdeen during Elphinstone's administration of the diocese. In the north aisle there are three effigies, only one of which can be identified. He is Walter Idill who died in the Chanonry some time between 1468 and 1472. The organ is a Willis of 1890, completely rebuilt in the 1920s. It is used for organ recitals and the Cathedral is often used now for concerts.

As you come out of the churchyard, the house opposite, No 13 the Chanonry, is the residence of the Principal of Aberdeen University. It dates from the 18th century with early 19th-century additions. A 17th-century map of Aberdeen by Parson Gordon of Rothiemay, which the Art Gallery has reproduced, shows the long gardens behind the Chanonry houses. At the corner of the Chanonry as you turn again there is the back entrance to Dunbar Hall, one of the University student residences, built on the original site of the Bishop's Palace and named after Bishop Dunbar. The buildings, designed by George Dunn and completed in 1967, were later awarded a Civic Design Award. They were planned sympathetically to fit in with the Cathedral and the older buildings in the area. On the left at the end of this stretch of the Chanonry is Chaplain's Court. Part of the building dates from the 16th century and has the arms of Bishop Dunbar, 'Argent, three cushions gules within the royal tressure'. The three-storey building is partly rubble and partly dressed granite with a crow-stepped roof.

Turn right into Don Street which has, on the right-hand side, attractive rows of small houses, most of them restored by the University. Looking briefly to the left, you can see the harled Bishop's Court and in Clark's Lane alongside it three attractive restored cottages. On the left, walking back towards St Machar Drive, is the University Chaplain's Manse set back in a garden. At the top of the street after a modern tenement block is Bede House, No 20-22 Don Street, dating from 1676 and once used to house Bishop Dunbar's Charity for eight old men. There still are eight bedesmen who receive a monthly pension and salmon on two occasions in the year, although they no longer live in this house. Bede's Court at the top of the street provides newer accommodation for the elderly.

Cross over St Machar Drive again and by the Town House catch a No 20 bus back to the city centre.

1. Wooden Bridge over the River Don
2. Grandholm Works
3. Donside Mills
4. Wallace Tower
5. Seaton Park
6. Motte of Tillydrone
7. Hillhead of Seaton —
   University Residences and Flats
8. Chapter House
9. Brig House
10. Brig o' Balgownie
11. Cot Town of Balgownie
12. New Bridge of Don
13. Royal Balgownie Golf-course

Route 10

River Don

Ellon Rd.

King Street

Don Street

River Don

THE RIVER DON FROM GRANDHOLM MILL
TO THE RIVERMOUTH

TAKE A NO 25 BUS FOR TILLYDRONE FROM THE bus stop outside St Nicholas Church in Union Street. The bus turns almost immediately into St Nicholas Street and its continuation George Street. The pleasant old shops are being allowed to decay in preparation for the building of a shopping precinct. On the right the stepped concrete building of the Northern Co-operative Society must surely rate as one of the most ill-conceived modern buildings in the city. At the end of George Street there are attractive granite cottages with gardens in front, before the bus swings into Bedford Road, with the old railway station at Kittybrewster on the left. The road goes along behind the University buildings with on the right the New University Library and another view of the Chemistry and Natural Philosophy Buildings and on the left school playing fields. The bus then crosses St Machar Drive into Tillydrone Avenue, and after meandering through a housing estate reaches the terminus above the Don.

Walk back a few yards until you see a wooden bridge across the Don. The view up and down the river from this point is worth several minutes' pause especially in autumn. On the other side of the river are the Grandholm Works of Messrs J. and J. Crombie Ltd, producers of some of the finest-quality cloth in Great Britain. The firm moved here from Cothal in 1859. Educational visits can be arranged if the request is made in advance and the Mill Shop is open on weekdays.

Come back across the bridge and climb the steps up to the road again, following the bus on its return to the city. On the left you pass the Donside Paper Company Ltd at the Donside Mills. This is one of a group of paper mills which cluster on the banks of the Don. Davidson and Sons are at Mugiemoss Works, Bucksburn, and Wiggins Teape at Stoney-wood, both on the other side of the river. The paper industry has been long established, both on the Don and the Dee, and the works are worth visiting, although the factory buildings are not of especial historic interest.

Walk along Tillydrone Road bearing to the left towards Seaton Park. On the right stands the Wallace Tower, a Z-plan tower used as a town residence in the 17th century by the Keiths of Benholm. It originally stood in the Netherkirkgate, below St Nicholas Church, but was moved stone by stone to its new resting-place in the 1960s when Marks and Spencer's shop was built. The name Wallace appears not to belong to the historical figure, but is a corruption of 'well house' from the water supply in the Netherkirkgate.

The road then leads on to the corner of the Chanonry with St Machar Cathedral ahead. Turn left into Seaton Park. This must be one of the most splendid open spaces that any city can boast. High above on the left as you walk down towards the Don is the motte of Tillydrone, the remaining earthwork of an 11th-century, timber-built castle which would have commanded this part of the river against invaders from all sides. The Don flows broadly over boulders in this open stretch of the park, before narrowing into a gorge on its way to the sea. The path becomes steeper and wooded, following a wide sweep of the river, before coming out into Don Street above the Brig o' Balgownie. Before following it, return to the centre of the park and the pleasant flower beds. The formal mansion of the Hays of Seaton, built in 1715, supposedly to the plans of the architect James Gibb, was burnt down in 1963. Climbing up the steps to the plateau above the centre borders you find the complex of University residences and flats at Hillhead of Seaton. Either join Don Street here, or retrace your steps along the woodland path by the river.

As you emerge from the latter, you pass an L-shaped 17th-century house called the Chapter House. It is too far from the Chanonry to have served such a function, but it may have been constructed from some of the material from buildings there. The initials and the coat of arms on the pend arch are those of George Cruickshank of Berriehill, and his wife, Barbara Hervie of Elrick, who had the house built. The date 1655 is probably that of the completion of the building. Lower down the hill on the right is the Brig House, built on two levels, directly overlooking the bridge.

The bridge, a single span with a pointed Gothic arch, 60 feet high at the centre and 72 feet wide at the river level, is heavily buttressed on its southern approach. The date at which building began is uncertain, but it was finished by 1329. Some writers have seen in the similarity between the arch and the keep at Drum Castle, known to be the work of Richard the Mason, evidence that this early Provost of Aberdeen built the bridge too. The poet, Thomas the Rhymer, wrote a prophecy about the fate of the bridge which fortunately was not fulfilled.

Brig o' Balgownie, wicht's thy wa?
Wi' a wife's ae son an' a mare's ae foal
Doon shalt thou fa'.

In 1605 Sir Alexander Hay of Whytburgh endowed a Bridge Fund for its upkeep. The money accrued so handsomely that the new Bridge of Don was built in 1630 entirely from the interest. A plaque on the bridge commemorates his gift of £27.8.8 (Scots) 'for the love he had of the common good'.

On the other side of the bridge is the Cot Town of Balgownie, a community of but-and-ben cottages which have been well-restored. The one nearest to the Brig, the Black Nook, dates from 1600. Continuing down the Balgownie Road you meet the Ellon Road, a continuation of King Street. To the right is the new Bridge of Don, built in 1827-30 by the engineers John Smith and Thomas Telford. It was widened in 1958-60. It has seven spans of dressed stone with semi-hexagonal pedestrian niches. Crossing the road a little to the left of the bridge you pass the Coastguard Station and the

Round House and then reach the Royal Balgownie Golf course with the broad mouth of the River Don on the right. Come back to the Ellon Road and catch a No 1, 2 or 3 bus back to the centre of the city.

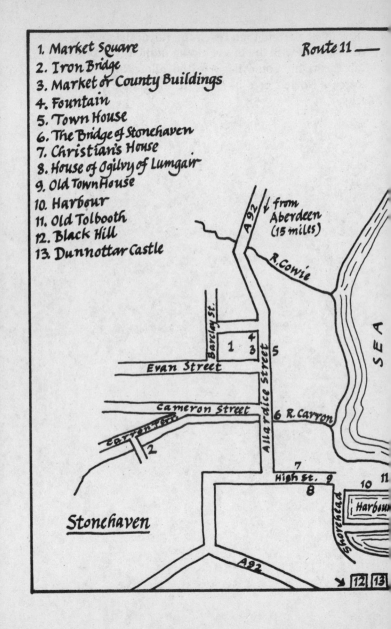

1. Market Square
2. Iron Bridge
3. Market or County Buildings
4. Fountain
5. Town House
6. The Bridge of Stonehaven
7. Christian's House
8. House of Ogilvy of Lumgair
9. Old Town House
10. Harbour
11. Old Tolbooth
12. Black Hill
13. Dunnottar Castle

Route 11 ——

↓ from Aberdeen (15 miles)

R. Cowie

SEA

Barclay St.

A 92

1   4
    3   5

Evan Street

Cameron Street

Carron St.

2

Allardice Street

6 R. Carron

7

High St. 9

8

10   11

Harbour

Shorehead

A 92

→ 12 13

Stonehaven

Route 11

STONEHAVEN AND DUNNOTTAR

THE ROAD TO THE SOUTH OF ABERDEEN follows the high cliffs of the coastline towards Stonehaven which is a natural harbour, sixteen miles away on the edge of the Highland fault. South again you reach the open farmland of the Howe o' the Mearns, the country of Lewis Grassic Gibbon's trilogy of novels, *Sunset Song, Cloud Howe* and *Grey Granite; A Scots Quair* as the works are known collectively. A train journey to Stonehaven gives you the best view of the indentation of the coastline, the height of the cliffs and the colonies of sea birds, but Alexander's buses run hourly from the bus station near the main railway station. However, if you want to go on to Dunnottar Castle a car is the easiest way of getting beyond Stonehaven on the coast road.

Light industry is stretching out of Aberdeen on this side, and south clifftop villages like Portlethen show their mark. In the past twenty years Newtonhill has become a dormitory town for Aberdeen. The bus weaves in and out of the small communities before rejoining the main road to Stonehaven.

The town lies in a hollow of the cliffs, and one of the attractions of this rather stern place is the sight of the two main rivers, the Cowie and the Carron, and other small rivulets winding their way to the sea. The northern side of the town has been developed for the summer visitor with a caravan site, a swimming pool, and a new hotel on the west side of the road. Notice as you cross the bridge into Stonehaven the row of rubble granite cottages on the southern side of the Cowie River. The main road to the south drives relentlessly through Allardice Street, cutting the town into two.

The western side of the town is laid out in a grid plan round the large Market Square, dominated by the Market Building with its steeple. This New Town of Stonehaven was laid out in 1793 by Robert Barclay. The Old Statistical Account noted 'he has laid down by a regular plan twelve acres of ground with streets forty-eight feet wide and a square of two acres'. Robert Barclay's son, Robert Barclay-Allardice, and other members of the family gave their names to streets in the town, such as Allardice Street, Barclay Street, Ann Street and Cameron Street. The buildings were mixed, terraced houses and shops near the square, with detached houses with gardens further up the braes to the west.

The shops, in spite of the addition of a few chain-store fronts, retain a pleasant country-town appearance. On the corner of Evan Street and Barclay Street is the old-fashioned grocery shop, Thomas Mitchell, founded in 1856, and further up on the south side of Evan Street is E. Giulianotti, established in 1899, a most incredible sweet shop, selling chocolates and sweets from all over the world. Further to the south, where Cameron Street joins Carron Terrace, an attractive decorated iron bridge, built in 1879, crosses the Carron Water.

Return to the Market Square. The Market or County Buildings were put up in 1826. The money for the clock tower and the steeple was raised by public subscription. The bell in the steeple is inscribed 'Spire, Clock and Bell erected by Town Council of Newtown and Stonehaven by subscription, 1857'. The fountain in the north-east corner of the square was presented by George Barrie in 1897, and is constructed of four different types of granite: Aberdeen, Kemnay, Peterhead and Norwegian.

Cross busy Allardice Street. Opposite the Market Buildings is the Royal Hotel (1827) and the Town House built in Renaissance style in 1878, again by public subscription. Here too is the Thomson Reading Room, again a pleasant 19th-century survival. A plaque proclaims 'The Birthplace of William Thomson, the Inventor of the Pneumatic Tyre, born 29th June 1822. Died 8th March 1873'. His patent proclaimed 'The nature of my invention consists in the application of elastic bearings around the tyres of the wheels of carriages, rendering their motion easier, and diminishing the noise they make when in motion. I prefer employing for the purpose a hollow belt composed of some air and watertight material such as caoutchouc or gutta percha, and inflating it with air, whereby, the wheels will, in every part of their revolution present a cushion of air to the ground, or rail, or track on which they return'.

Keep on this east side of Allardice Street and walk south. At the end the main road takes a sharp turn to the west. Across the road you can see the old Mill Inn, a former coaching stop. Just west of it are the remains of the town's Meal Mill. The Bridge of Stonehaven, which divides the old and the new towns, was built by Robert Barclay in 1781, but widened with footpaths of iron girders in 1885, and widened again in 1973. The inscription on the south approach is a copy of the one on the 1781 bridge and records the names of members of the Barclay family.

Turn left towards the sea along the High Street, the main street of the Old Town. Some old houses remain, but much has been rebuilt, although the new buildings fit sympathetically into the closely-huddled groups of old houses. The first wynd to the left has an old cooper's workshop with a roof of stone flags. Back in the High Street is Christian's House (Nos 28-32 High Street). Built in 1712, it has a portico with ornate pillars. A crown lantern hangs over the front door. Further down on the right is the former St James Episcopal School opened in 1851. The belfry still exists at the back.

Cross back to the left side and walk beyond the King Street turning. There you will see the Water Yett, or Water Gate, which leads to the River Carron and the sea. It would previously have been closed by a portcullis. On the opposite side of the road is No 51 High Street, known as the House of Ogilvy of Lumgair. It dates from the early 17th century. A projecting circular tower is corbelled out in the middle of the building above the first floor and contains the upper staircase. Further down the street on the south side is the Old Town House, a square building built in 1790 with a Flemish-style roof capped by a steeple. A bell and a clock tower were added three years later, and in 1894 the clock tower was raised a floor and the clock was given a new dial. The unusual large barometer which hangs from the steeple was put up in 1852. The shaft of the old Mercat Cross at the foot of the building dates from the middle of the 17th century, but the top was replaced to celebrate Queen Victoria's Jubilee in 1887.

From here it is a short walk to the harbour, deeply set at the base of the red sandstone cliffs of the Bervie Braes, and sheltered even in stormy weather. The 'old pier' which forms the North Harbour was commissioned by George, ninth Earl Marischal, in 1700, and it remained the only part enclosed until 1812 when the engineer Robert Stevenson, Robert Louis' grandfather, was asked to plan the Southern Harbour by the construction of a South Pier and two basins. The work was begun in 1826, and in 1837 it was completed with the west jetty, extending from the point of the South Pier.

The Shorehead is a curved street of well-kept buildings at sea level. The Ship Inn dates from 1711 and the Marine Hotel from the late 19th century. The grotesque corbel heads in the walls of the latter come from Dunnottar Castle. Wallace Wynd leads up to the restored Castle Square, which won a Saltire Society Award for its imaginative new housing. Back at the harbour, the most noteworthy building is the Old Tolbooth on the Old Pier. It is built of red sandstone with crow-stepped gables and dates from 1710. It was built originally probably as a warehouse and later turned into a prison. When the New Town building took over this function, it reverted to its old use, but eventually fell into disrepair. The building was restored in 1963 and now houses a Museum of Local History.

Return now to the bridge and take the road south out of the town. By the former Invercarron Toll House take the left fork, the A92. On the right is the Black Hill with a classical-style war memorial on the top. There is a magnificent, perhaps the best, view of Stonehaven New Town from the top. Continue along the road and some two miles from Stonehaven you reach the promontory of Dunnottar. The name itself means 'Place of strength', and the site of the castle surrounded on three sides by sheer cliffs is one of the most impressive in the British Isles.

A castle seems to have existed here from the time of William the Lion (1165-1214), and from the end of the 14th century it was one of the strongholds of the Earls Marischal of Scotland. In 1651 the castle was besieged by Cromwell's men, and the Crown, Sword and Sceptre were smuggled out of the castle by two women. In 1685 167 Covenanters were imprisoned in the castle, many dying from the treatment they received. The Covenanters' Stone in Dunnottar Kirkyard was being restored by one Robert Paterson when Sir Walter Scott visited the place and he became the novelist's 'Old Mortality'.

The entrance to the castle is by a tunnel in the rock. Stone steps lead to the main entrance. The

30-feet curtain wall is 7 feet 6 inches thick with a building on the right, known as Benholm's Lodging, five storeys high with crow-stepped gables. Enter by the Gatehouse which dates from 1575 and walk through the Magazine, the Guard Room and the Barrack Room. This extremely well-fortified entrance protected the castle's weakest flank.

The Keep stands on the south-west corner of the rock. It is an L-shaped building about 50 feet long with 5 feet-thick rubble walls. It has a kitchen and store at the basement level, and the Great Hall on the first floor with a private room at the side. The Upper Hall is on the third storey and a spiral staircase leads from this to the battlemented caphouse and parapet wall. The range of ruined buildings to the east of the keep were a store house, a smithy and the stables. The detached house to the north of the last building is known as the Priest's House next to the Kirkyard.

The Great Quadrangle on the north-east of the rock was built over a period of a hundred years from the 16th to the 17th centuries. The range called the Seven Chambers is the oldest. The north range was a kitchen with a dining-room above with the Marischal's rooms to the east, and the Countess' Rooms near the Chapel to the west. The third range contained the brew house and the bakery. There is a circular well, 31 feet in diameter, in the courtyard.

The castle was acquired in 1919 by the Cowdray family and Lady Cowdray began the restoration of the ruins in 1925. The property is now administered by the Scottish Development Department and is open every day from 9.00—5.00 pm and from 2.00—5.00 pm on Sundays.

The total distance for this round trip is about 36 miles.

1. Pitmedden Great Garden
2. Old Meldrum
3. Pitcaple Castle
4. Inverurie
5. The Bass
6. Inverurie Paper Mills
7. Kintore

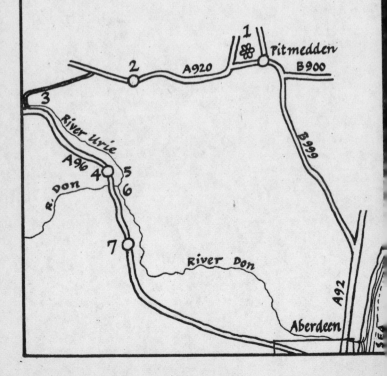

PITMEDDEN, PITCAPLE AND INVERURIE

IF YOU WANT TO DO THIS ROUTE BY BUS IT means two expeditions, one to Pitmedden itself, and the other to Inverurie and Pitcaple. By car the whole route, a round trip of about 68 miles, makes a satisfactory afternoon's journey.

Leave Aberdeen by the A92 to Newton of Murcar about two miles north of the Bridge of Don. Turn left along the B999 and then go along the B900, to Pitmedden, turning left again in the village to Pitmedden Great Garden.

The National Trust has owned this property since 1952. The estate had been owned by the Seton family from 1603-1899. In the latter year the Keiths acquired it, and it was Major James Keith (1879-1903) who began the restoration of the garden. A fire in 1818 had destroyed much of the old house and its records, so there was no plan of the original Great Garden. Scotland has few formal gardens; Edzell Castle in Angus, smaller but much better preserved, is the only other one in the north-east. After the National Trust took over, Dr J. S. Richardson, the Trust's expert on landscape gardening, consulted Gordon of Rothiemay's description of Holyrood Palace Garden to redesign the lower sunken part of Pitmedden.

You go in through a pillared entrance in the middle of the upper wall and walk down steps to the lower level, a sunken square of 475 feet. The borders are fringed with box hedging and yew. The most elaborate section is the north-western bed which was designed as a tribute to an earlier owner, Sir Alexander Seton, who died in the service of Charles I. His coat of arms, the Scottish saltire and thistle, and the motto, 'Sustento sangine signa' (I bear the standards with blood), are picked out with bedding plants. The patterns in the other three sections are based on the Holyroodhouse designs. The centre piece of the garden is a sundial, contemporary with the old house, surrounded with paths of coloured pebbles and stones from local rivers. The herbaceous borders were planned by Lady Burnett who was also responsible for much of the planting at Crathes Castle (see Route 13).

The high walls which surround the garden are covered with espaliered trees and climbing plants. The two pavilions at the north and south ends of the west wall have been restored. The northern one is in the best state of preservation. The lower apartment is entered from the Great Garden level and has a rib-vaulted room which houses an attractive photographic exhibition, devised by the National Trust, on the development of the formal garden in the British Isles. The upper apartment is a small summer-house.

Climb the steps again to the upper garden which gives, perhaps, the best view of the formal patterns below The upper garden has been levelled and planted, one section being devoted to a herb garden which is still being extended. A nearby barnyard houses a small collection of old agricultural implements.

Pitmedden Great Garden is open throughout the year. It is at its most spectacular in summer when the thousands of plants are in flower, but the formal arrangement is interesting even in winter.

Return to the B900 and continue to Old Meldrum. Through the village turn left along the minor road to Fingask and Mill of Pitcaple. The road skirts the Pitcaple Estate, but the entrance to Pitcaple Castle is on the A96 (turn left towards Aberdeen).

The castle, which is still privately-owned by the Burges-Lumsden family, is open from 9.00 am to 6.00 pm for most of the year. (It is advisable to phone in advance in the winter months to confirm the opening times.) You will be shown round by Captain or Mrs Burges-Lumsden whose care and affection for the place is evident everywhere. The earliest part of the building is a 15th-century, Z-plan tower house, with two diagonally-placed towers at the opposite corners of a rectangular fortress. A charter of 1457, on view in the museum room, gave the castle and the lands to the Leslie family, and they retained it until 1757 when Jane Leslie married John Lumsden and united the property to that of another notable north-eastern family.

The Edinburgh architect, William Burn, was employed to add a more comfortable wing in 1830. This part of the house is entered through a massive 12 feet-high doorway into a hall with granite pillars, and then to fine reception rooms where the family's furniture and pictures are on view. The gunloops of the tower have been opened up, the rooms furnished and, at the top, the family has created a very attractive museum of documents and objects concerning the history of the castle and the families who have owned it. There are charters and estate documents as well as clothes and domestic memorabilia.

Come back towards Aberdeen through Inverurie, a spacious small town, built where the River Ury joins the Don. The town was important for its Railway Works, built in 1898-1905 by the engineer William Pickersgill for the Great North of Scotland Railway. (British Rail is still an employer in the town.) There are a number of steel-framed, granite-clad workshops. Workers' houses of the same period also exist; six blocks of two-storey granite houses. The station was also rebuilt at the same time.

Leaving the town you see on your left, the Bass, a 50-feet-high conical mound covered with grass, with a smaller mound, the Little Bass, beside it. It was the site of a motte and bailey castle which would have had a wooden structure on top. There is an interesting Pictish stone in the grounds. Further on on the same side you pass the Inverurie Paper Mills down on the Don. These were built in 1858 and the complex of buildings is dominated by a five-storey brick tower.

Next you go through Kintore, formerly a very small royal burgh, now developing rapidly with new housing estates. The Town House (1740), on the right as you leave the town, has two curved flights of stone steps, a clock tower and an ogival slated roof.

Return to Aberdeen through Bucksburn and Woodside.

1. Banchory
2. Crathes Castle
3. Deeside Railway ---- (abandoned)
4. Nature Trail

Aberdeen→
A 93

Island of Dee

A 943
Aberdeen→

A 93

Crathes Dee
River

A 943

4
2
4

River Dee

Bridge
of
Feugh

Bridge
of Dee

1

3

CRATHES CASTLE,
GARDENS AND WOODLAND TRAIL

THIS ROUTE CAN BEGIN IN ABERDEEN EITHER
by taking a Banchory or Ballater bus from the bus
station and getting off at Crathes Castle itself or by
going on to Banchory and walking the two and a
half miles back to the house along the track of the
former Deeside Railway, now abandoned.

The castle is owned now by the National Trust for
Scotland, and the house is only open from the
beginning of April to the end of September. The
grounds and the Nature Trail are open throughout
the year.

Crathes Castle remained in the same family, that
of the Burnetts of Leys, from the middle of the 16th
century, and they had been eminent in the area
from the time of Robert the Bruce. The ninth laird
began the building in 1553, and it was finished just
before the turn of the century. The family con-
solidated its lands in Kincardineshire, and in 1619
began building another residence nearer the coast,
the Castle of Muchalls.

The fact of its continued occupation by one
family for its own use gives Crathes a special

interest in the choice of furniture and furnishings, and the decoration which reflects the family's taste over many generations. The house is a six-storied tower, built on a variation of the L-plan, extending 43 feet by 50 feet. There is a corbelled turret stair from the second floor up. The building is crowned with round and square turrets, decorated with gargoyles and ornate decoration on the dormer windows. A later residential wing added in the 18th century was damaged badly by fire a few years ago.

Go in through the tower doorway and up the spiral staircase to the Great Hall. This huge vaulted room would have been the heart of the tower house. The large window was added in 1800. Originally there was a dais in front of the fireplace to accommodate the laird's own table for the family and their guests. The pendants from the ceiling display the Burnett arms, three holly leaves and a hunting horn. The original Ivory Horn of Leys is in a glass case above the fireplace. It was reputedly given by Robert the Bruce to Alexander Burnett with the lands of Crathes in 1323, and was a mark of the office Burnett held as Coroner of the Royal Forest of Drum. Under the agreement made with the National Trust it is never to leave the castle. The hall has traces of the original painted plaster in the arched window bays which show the arms of Alexander Burnett, the ninth laird who began the building, and his wife, Janet Hamilton, and those of Alexander Burnett, the twelfth laird who completed it, and his wife Katherine Gordon. Also in the hall is an oak chest with carved portraits of the latter two and five family portraits by George Jamesone, one of the earliest Scottish portrait painters, and a native of Aberdeen. Traces also remain of a 'Laird's Lug', or listening tube to the staircase outside. It was convenient for testing the loyalty of guests.

The floor above the Great Hall has been divided into two bedrooms. They have the original pine floorboards, laid at the time of the building of the castle. In the second room Alexander Burnett and Katherine Gordon's four poster bed survives, dated 1594 and with its original hangings. Their arms and carved portraits appear on this too. The oak wardrobe with their initials ABKG also stands in this room.

On the floor above is the Chamber of the Nine Nobles with its fine tempera painted ceiling, which was obscured in later centuries and not properly restored until 1962-3. The nine 'worthies' are three pagan heroes, Hector of Troy, Alexander the Great and Julius Caesar; three old testament heroes, Joshua, David and Judas Maccabaeus and three Christian heroes, Arthur, Charlemagne and Godfrey of Bouillon, one of the leaders of the First Crusade.

Each hero has a verse describing his exploits. King David's is as follows:

> For wit and manheid David was maid king,
> From Schepirds rank over Israell to ring,
> He slew the gryt Goliath hand to hand,
> And did gryt damage to the heathen land.

The verses end with the question:

> Seeze not thy harte on welth or earthlie gains,

They perish suine but honor still remains.
Gude reader tell me or thou pas
Whilk of thir nyn maist valliant was.

Heraldic animals and symbols are interspersed among the figures and the ceiling is dated 1602.

Next door is the Green Room said to be haunted by a girl in green carrying a baby. It also has a painted ceiling but the motifs have no particular theme. The furniture in these two rooms is on loan from various museums.

The Long Gallery runs the length of the top floor. It has an oak-panelled ceiling, unique in Scotland, with embossed coats of arms, among which are the Royal Arms of Scotland. The barony court would have been held here. At the east end is a small domestic chapel.

Coming down again you reach the Chamber of the Nine Muses, decorated with another fine ceiling representing the Muses and five Virtues, Wisdom, Justice, Faith, Hope and Charity. There are more verses attached to these figures. The arms of Alexander and Katherine Burnett appear again and the date 1599.

Down further to the level of the Guest Hall you pass through the Stone Hall, a small withdrawing room which is furnished in 16th-century style. Note particularly the chairs with coats of arms and initials and the date 1597 on Katherine Gordon's chair.

Outside the castle you can visit the formal gardens designed in the early 18th century. Less symbolic in their arrangement than Pitmedden, they really form a series of outdoor 'rooms', each one different in character. Lady Burnett developed the planting in the 1930s, introducing numbers of rare shrubs and herbaceous plants designed to provide interest at every season of the year. Adjoining the house is a lawn and a garden with formal hedged beds round a pool at one end, which gives it its name of the Pool Garden. Borders flank the wall and the yew hedge, which form two sides of the space. The yew hedges, planted in 1702, now reach a height of over twelve feet, and divide the Fountain Garden and the Rose Garden, also laid out formally.

The rest of the garden is divided into four more 'rooms', the Camel and the Trough Garden at the top, leading to the last two, closely planted with shrubs and flowers. The herbaceous borders which flank these gardens have been created to make a special display, such as the White Border and the June Border.

Further out into the policies, a woodland Nature Trail has been made. The 575 acres given with the castle include 400 acres of woodland, much of which had to be replanted after the storms of 1953. The woodland Nature Trail, marked by wooden posts, is about two miles long, although it is possible to do a shorter version. An attractive feature of the walk is the mixture of native trees and imported species. The walk begins at the lime tree path by the garden wall. Just beyond the second post is a Ginkgo tree. The trail then passes the old Oak Wood of Crathes, of which some trees are over 200 years old. This woodland habitat of bracken, fern, foxglove and wood anenome provides a home for robins, blackbirds, song thrushes, mistle thrushes, tree creepers and tits.

Between posts 15 and 24 you get open glimpses of the parkland. Walk along the main water track which supplies Aberdeen. You can often see curlews and oyster catchers on this stretch of the route.

You then go through an old sand quarry which provides another type of plant habitat producing broom and plants which like dry soil. Post 33 is suggested as the point at which you can turn if you have had enough of natural history. The walk goes on through the glen of the Burn of Coy, a tributary of the Dee. A dam forms a mill pond for a mill further down. The lake is an ornamental one enlarged from a natural loch at the beginning of the 19th century. You can see wildfowl such as duck and moorhens here. The bridge crossing the road is a good point for watching salmon and sea trout leaping in the autumn.

Oak and larch plantings lead up the glen, and Wellingtonias have also matured. There is a view of the castle between posts 43 and 44. The route then goes through a marshy area with a stream running by and then through a rhododendron thicket to another glen, clad with broom and gorse in the summer. Woodland birds can again be seen (and heard) here. At post 66 follow a haha along two fields to further woods, mostly coniferous with the older Douglas firs and the newer quicker-growing Norway Spruce. The route then ends at the drive by the kitchen garden.

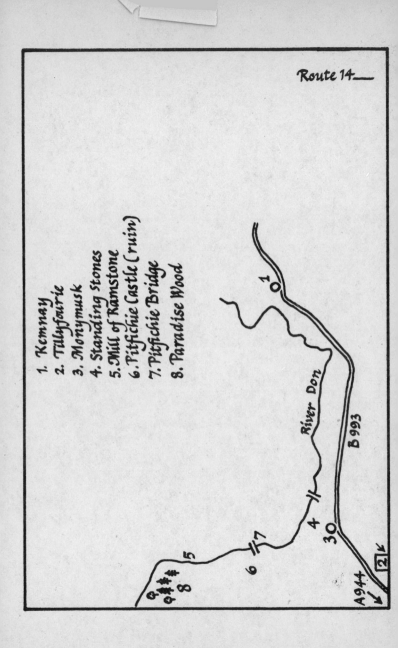

1. Kemnay
2. Tillyfourie
3. Monymusk
4. Standing Stones
5. Mill of Ramstone
6. Pitfichie Castle (ruin)
7. Pitfichie Bridge
8. Paradise Wood

MONYMUSK

THIS EXPEDITION TAKES YOU INTO THE
heart of Aberdeenshire where its most famous
mountain, Bennachie, watches over fertile
farmland and wooded landscape.

The bus from Aberdeen to Monymusk goes via,
Kemnay, now developed as a dormitory town for
Aberdeen and formerly most renowned for its
granite quarry which was one of the chief sources
of supply for the building of Aberdeen. By car you
can leave Aberdeen by the A944, past the Loch of
Skene and Dunecht (see Route 17), turning off by
Tillyfourie to Monymusk. An alternative route is to
go out of the city by the A96 to the north, turning
off along the B994 just before you reach Kintore.
You then follow this road to Kemnay and from
there take the B993 to Monymusk.

The village was planned and the surrounding
area developed by Sir Archibald Grant, second
Baronet of Monymusk, whose descendants still
own the 'big' house, which is not open to the public.
He inherited the house from his father, an
Edinburgh lawyer, who had not devoted much time
to estate management. His son regarded his

inheritance somewhat ruefully at first, writing in 1713, 'The house was an old castle with battlements and six different roofs of various heights and directions, confusedly and inconveniently combined, and all rotten, with two wings more modern, of two storeys only, the half of the windows of the higher rising above the roofs, with granaries, stables and houses for all cattle, and of the vermine attending them, close adjoining, and with the heath and the muire reaching in angles or goushets to the gate, and much heath near, and what land near was in culture belonging to the farmers, by which their cattle and dung were always at the door. The whole land raised and uneven and full of stones, many of them very large, of a hard iron quality, and all the ridges crooked in the shape of an S, and very high and full of noxious weeds and poor, being worn out by culture, without proper manure or tillage. . . . The people poor, ignorant and slothfull, and ingrained enimies to planting, inclosing or any improvements or cleanness'.

He set out to drain the marshy area by the River Don, to enclose lands and improve the system of farming by developing the fallow system which rested and enriched the soil. The 'drystane dykes', or drystone walls, which he built, can still be seen in many of the fields near the village. He built up a big farm at the Mains of Monymusk to show his improved farming in practice. His tenants were not very impressed at first and retaliated by uprooting newly-planted trees.

Monymusk House lies north-east of the church,

on the banks of the Don. The central L-shaped tower dates from 1587 and was built by William Forbes, a member of the family, who owned the estate before the Grants. The house was extended in the 18th century. The church in the village is the oldest existing building in the area. A chapel here was said to have belonged to some of the earliest Scottish missionaries. In 1170 Gilchrist, Earl of Mar endowed an Augustinian priory on the site which existed until the Reformation. When the Forbes family bought the land they turned the priory chapel into the parish church and retained the dedication to St Mary. The building is of pink granite with decorations of Kildrummy sandstone. At the west end there is a solid square crenellated tower which once had a spire. Inside you can see the Norman arches and the original choir which was restored in 1932. The stained glass windows and the wrought ironwork are modern, and the church has many memorials to the Grant family. There are also two Pictish stones propped against the wall, one bearing a wheel cross, the other a swastika.

The church also owns some fine 17th- and 18th-century silver, and a rich series of parish records dating from 1678. Its most famous treasure is the Monymusk Reliquary, a 7th-century casket which held a bone of St Columba. It belonged to the priory, was then transferred to Monymusk House, but is now in the Museum of Antiquities in Edinburgh.

The village houses cluster round a large green. Monymusk is one of the few northern Scottish villages planned in this way. The houses, designed as model dwellings for the estate tenants, were built in the early 19th century, and they have recently been modernised. One is now a craft shop so it is possible to see the panelled interior and the solidly-built room. On the east side, is Lord Cullen's School, now a hall, but formerly the school built by Sir Archibald Grant's father for the estate children. A mill with a dam and pond stands to the north-west of the village. On the opposite side of the road from these are three standing stones.

Continue along this road, past the Mill of Ramstone, a mid-19th-century corn mill, a rectangular rubble building with a lean-to wheel house for a low breast wheel. About a mile from Monymusk you come to the ruined Castle of Pitfichie, a rectangular building with a large round tower, dating from the late 16th century. The bridge at Pitfichie is a 1906 girder construction by James Abernethy and Co of Aberdeen.

A mile further on is the entrance to Paradise Wood, stocked with mature oaks, larches and conifers. It was laid out as a wooded park in 1719 by Lord Cullen. The Grants are supposed to have planted more trees than anyone else in Britain at that time, 'fifty million in fifty years'. It is worth coming on a fine day and walking here.

The road further on narrows, with overhanging branches and has the attractive name of the Lord's Throat. Return to Monymusk where the hotel does a good tea.

By car from Aberdeen to Monymusk and return is a trip of about 56 miles.

1. Balmedie
2. Ellon
3. Newburgh
4. The Sands of Forvie
5. Collieston
6. Bullers O'Buchan
7. Cruden Bay

Peterhead

A92

A975

River Ythan

Aberdeen A92

SEA

NEWBURGH AND THE BULLERS O' BUCHAN

THIS EXPEDITION IS PRIMARILY FOR THE natural history enthusiast, although the industrial archaeologist may see some things of interest.

Leave Aberdeen by the A92 Ellon Road. (There is a Newburgh bus from the Aberdeen bus station, but it is not possible to do the whole of the route by one bus. With a car this route is a round trip of 40 miles.) About eight miles out of Aberdeen you pass the turning to Balmedie, a splendid stretch of beach and dunes. Five miles further north turn off to the right on to the A975 to Newburgh.

This village, like many others within commuting distance of Aberdeen, has become popular with the building of new estates. It lies at the mouth of the River Ythan, which once provided a navigable waterway up to Ellon. In the village are the remains of an 18th-century warehouse, probably a granary, two-storeys high with an attic, built in harled rubble. There are traces too of a rubble-built quay. At the north end of the village, at Culterty, stands a three-storey brick-built mill, with a kiln, now also in ruins. Beside it is a three-storey, twenty-bay, wood and iron-framed, corrugated-iron granary, built in

1897 by Spencer and Co of Melkham, Wiltshire. There are also remains of rubble-built warehouses and another quay.

The village church was originally a chapel of ease, built in 1882, with a burial ground on a small promontory called Inches, which juts out into the river just north of the village. The Udny family, who owned the castles of Udny and Knockhall in the north-east, were buried here. To the south of the village by the links are an old vaulted ice house formerly used for storing fish, and also an old lifeboat station.

The area is most famous, however, for bird-watching and for the dune habitat with its distinctive flora. The Sands of Forvie, across the Ythan, stretch north nearly as far as Collieston, and are a Nature Conservancy Reserve. The area has the largest colony of eider duck in the British Isles, four different species of terns, and at appropriate times of year vast flocks of migrating wildfowl on their way to or from the north.

The dunes cover the remains of a stone age village of nineteen circular huts, about two thousand years old, which were excavated in 1951. The archaeologists also found traces of a lost medieval village. Excavations of the old Church of Forvie, alleged to have been founded by St Ninian, were begun in the last century but were never finished.

Back on the Newburgh side of the estuary, and to the north of the village is Culterty Field Station, left to Aberdeen University in the will of Dr H. Edgar Smith as a place for research in ornithology, botany and zoology. Although it is not open to the public, those with a special interest in birds would probably be allowed to visit if they phoned in advance (except in the breeding season).

Newburgh was the birthplace of James McBey, the artist (1884-1939). His autobiography describes the village nearly a century ago. 'Through a gap in the sand dunes lay the sea, flat, crouching and angry, thrashing itself on the sand to the edge of the world. Its steady muttering drone was the background of sound against the silence in which we all lived'. He later moved to Aberdeen to work in a bank, and taught himself to draw from books in the Public Library. He eventually became an Official War Artist in World War I, following Allenby's Expeditionary Force in Egypt. One of his best-known etchings, *Dawn: the Camel Patrol Setting Out,* as well as other desert scenes, may owe something to his early observations of the dunes at Newburgh.

Back on the A975 again, you cross the Ythan and about three and a half miles along the road you come to the turning on to the B903 leading to the small fishing port of Collieston, now primarily a holiday place. Further north beaches are left behind and the coast becomes rocky with high cliffs. The most spectacular are those at the Bullers O' Buchan, south of Peterhead.

Dr Johnson and Boswell visited them on their way north, as reported in *A Tour to the Hebrides.* After visiting Slains Castle, 'We got into the coach and drove to Dunbuy, a rock near the shore, just an island covered with seafowl. Then to a circular basin of large extent, surrounded with tremendous rocks. On the quarter to the sea there is a high arch in the rock which the force of the tempest has driven out. This place is called Buchan's Buller, or the Bullers of Buchan, and the country people call it the pot. Mr Boyd said it was so called from the French *bouilloire*. It may be more simply traced from *boiler* in our own language. We walked round this mountainous cauldron. In some places the rock is very narrow, and on each side you have a sea deep enough for a man-of-war to ride in, so that it is somewhat horrid to move along. However, there is earth and grass upon the rock, and a kind of road marked out by the print of feet, so that one makes it out pretty easily. It was rather alarming to see Mr Johnson poking his way. He insisted to take a boat and sail into the Pot. We did so. He was stout and wonderfully alert'.

The cliffs are covered with breeding colonies of puffin, guillemots and razorbills, and are pink with thrift in the summer.

From here return to Aberdeen, or if you are continuing north look at Route 18, Fraserburgh.

Route 16.

1. Deeside Railway - - - - (abandoned)
2. Banchory
3. Hill O'Fare
4. Kincardine O'Neil
5. Peel of Lumphanan
6. Aboyne
7. Forest of Birse
8. Ballater
9. Craigendarroch
10. Pass of Ballater
11. Lochnagar (3768 ft)
12. Crathie Church
13. Balmoral Castle
14. Braemar

Aberdeen

River Dee

THE DEE TO BRAEMAR

THIS ROUTE ALONG THE RIVER DEE RUNS through impressive mountain scenery and through several attractive small towns. A bus ride from Aberdeen is a peaceful way of seeing most of the sights mentioned in this journey, but a car would enable you to stop and look at bridges and buildings more closely and also to take an alternative road for part of the way back. The round distance is about 110 miles.

Leave Aberdeen by the A93 through the western suburbs of the city. Cults, Bieldside, Milltimber and Peterculter retain some identity as places in their own right, although they are now virtually joined to Aberdeen. As J. R. Allan put it, 'There are suburbs all the way to Culter; villas and bungalows of the people who have done well; while on the south side there are some bigger houses of the people who have done even better'.

At Cults you can see the St Devenick Bridge, built in 1836-7 by John Smith who also worked on the Aberdeen Wellington Suspension Bridge. It is similarly constructed with iron rod suspenders, iron rod chains and a wooden deck. The main span is 185 feet wide, but the south section has disappeared. At Culter there are the paper mills, dating from 1751. The main building is on an L-plan with three storeys and an attic of 16 by 27 bays, with Flemish gables on the front. The tall chimney is a notable landmark.

The Deeside Railway which used to run between Aberdeen and Ballater is now disused, but the old track provides excellent walks at various points in its length. The Cults-Culter section is one such short stretch, and Crathes to Banchory another. A more ambitious expedition would be the fifteen miles from Cults to Banchory.

The main road continues to Banchory, eighteen miles west of Aberdeen. The Hill O'Fare lies to the north. Like most of the towns along the Dee, Banchory developed from a small village with the advent of the railway in 1853. If you have a car, drive over the Bridge of Dee, south of the town, to the Bridge of Feugh, a late 18th-century structure, just above where a tributary joins the main river. The narrows create swift rapids which salmon leap in the autumn. Return to the main Braemar road.

The road follows the line of the river through wooded country. Kincardine O'Neil used to be important as the point where the old Cairn O'Mount road from the south came in, and there was a ferry crossing. The remains of a medieval church still stand in the churchyard. Just beyond the village a minor road to the north leads to the Peel of Lumphanan, an artificial motte, which like the Bass of Inverurie, would have had a wooden structure on top. A surrounding moat completed the castle's defence. North through the village is Macbeth's

Cairn, where Macbeth is alleged to have been buried before his body was removed to the royal burial place of Iona.

Return to the main road. The river makes a loop to the south and the road continues north-west to Aboyne. Aboyne is another town closely-connected with a family, in this case the Earls of Aboyne. Originally a settlement near the castle to the north, the present small town developed in the second half of the 19th century. The War Memorial and Victory Hall on the north side of the green are worth looking at. St Machar's Church in neo-Gothic style was built in 1842. The station, now closed, dates from 1859, although it was rebuilt at the beginning of the 20th century. It has two platforms and a single-storey granite building with pepper-pot turrets on the up side. Aboyne has annual Highland Games in September.

South of the River Dee from Aboyne lies the Forest of Birse, originally part of the old Caledonian Forest, but now only partly wooded. To the south-east, just over the river is the old Chapel of Birse, built in 1779. It is a low granite building with a stained glass window. It contains an inscribed stone, known as the Crusader Stone, dating from the 13th century, with a Maltese cross, a two-headed sword and a battle axe. The Forest is also of interest to the industrial archaeologist. There is a bucket mill, which was working up to a decade ago, the mid-19th-century Mill of Clinter with an overshot wheel, the Midstrath Limekiln of the last century, a turning works and the Potarch Bridge, built in 1811-13 by Thomas Telford.

Return to the A93. The road continues through Dinnet and Cambus O'May, which lie in a hollow of the Dee before the Highlands proper begin, to Ballater. This town, like Aboyne, has a green. It was the terminal station of the Deeside Railway, and it was the railway that brought the town prosperity, although the Farquharson family began the development in the 1770s. The granite Gothic church was begun at the end of the 18th century and rebuilt a century later. Its bell, which is much older, came from St Machar Cathedral in Aberdeen. Highland Games are held here too, in the Monaltrie Park at the north-east of the town. The Dee is very swift here, and the Bridge of Ballater records a series of disasters to previous structures.

To the north of the town is the hill of Craigendarroch, and the B972 leads through the Pass of Ballater, a deep defile through the mountains. To the south stretches Glen Muick (pronounced 'Mick'), from which the hardier can attempt the climb to Lochnagar (3768 ft). *Black's Guide to Scotland* (Pedestrians' Copy 1875) suggests, 'Those who are not accustomed to hard walking should avail themselves of Highland ponies, and choose a clear day for the ascent, as, on the whole the climb is a stony, boggy, and toilsome business'.

Return to the Deeside road which now reaches the 'royal' stretch of the country. Crathie Church, on the north side, was designed by A. Marshall Mackenzie (the architect of Marischal College, Aberdeen) in 1895. The church has memorials to members of the Royal Family. A small road behind

Crathie climbs to a height which gives a fine view of Balmoral Castle.

Balmoral Castle and its broad estates which include Loch Muick and Lochnagar are the personal property of the Queen. Prince Albert bought it in 1852 and employed William Smith, the Aberdeen architect, to rebuild the castle. The Scottish baronial building is in Invergelder granite from the estate, and has an 80 feet by 35 feet tower at the angle, linking two wings. The Castle is not open to the public, but the grounds may be visited in May, June and July, if the Royal Family is not in residence.

Continue along the main road to Braemar (1100 ft above sea level). The town is at the confluence of the Clunie and the Dee. The 18th-century Bridge and Mill of Clunie attract the artist as well as the industrial archaeologist. Braemar Castle stands about a mile to the east. It is a 17th-century L-plan house of five storeys with considerable later additions. Braemar itself is most famous for the Gathering held there every September. The athletic events include tossing the caber.

The road to the south of the town goes via the Devil's Elbow to Perth. To the west a minor road leads to Mar Lodge, said to have the largest collection of antlers anywhere, then to the small villages of Meikle and Little Inverey and beyond to the Linn of Dee, a deep gorge in the river. Beyond this, walking is really for the experienced, particularly through the Lairig Ghru Pass to Rothiemurcus and Speyside.

The bus will have stopped in Braemar and its

return journey is by the same route. The car driver can take the pleasant and quieter South Deeside road from Banchory (A943). The small church of Maryculter is worth looking at. Templars Park records the name of land which belonged to the Crusading Knights, first the Templars and then the Hospitallers. Further east is Blair's College, the Catholic college for training priests. It has a fine library, and two renowned portraits of Mary, Queen of Scots and Cardinal Beaton. Return to Aberdeen over the Bridge of Dee.

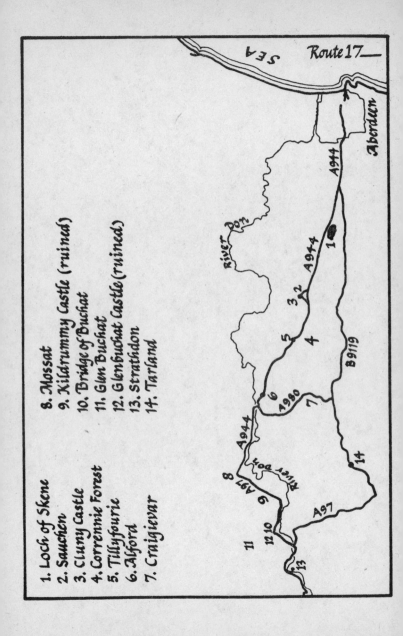

Route 17

SEA

Aberdeen

River Don

River Don

A944
A944
A944
A980
A97
A97
A91
B9119

1. Loch of Skene
2. Sauchen
3. Cluny Castle
4. Corrennie Forest
5. Tillyfourie
6. Alford
7. Craigievar

8. Mossat
9. Kildrummy Castle (ruined)
10. Bridge of Buchat
11. Glen Buchat
12. Glenbuchat Castle (ruined)
13. Strathdon
14. Tarland

Route 17

ABERDEEN TO STRATHDON

THIS EXPEDITION TAKES YOU ALONG Aberdeen's second river, the Don. The Dee and the Don tend to have their enthusiastic partisans, and I have to confess to preferring the latter. You can follow this route by the slow Strathdon bus which winds its way through hamlets and villages for a journey of over three hours to reach its destination. Travelling by car obviously gives you time to stop and look on the way.

Leave Aberdeen along the A944 which skirts Hazlehead Park and makes its way past the new dormitory town of Westhill. It is supposed to develop as a well-planned 'garden city', but it is still raw and unfinished. The bus winds its way through the housing estates and then rejoins the main road to go on to the Loch of Skene on the south side of the road. The two old villages of Kirkton of Skene and Lyne of Skene lie off the main road to the north.

The Loch of Skene is an impressive lake, nearly a mile in length. It is used for small-boat sailing. An ornate stone gateway to the estate can be seen from the road. Nearby, but hidden from view, stands Skene House, its core a tower house but with many additions. About two miles further along the road you come to the village of Dunecht with its 'big' house on the south side of the road. This is not visible from the road and is not open to the public. The estate belongs to Lord Cowdray. On the north side of the road you can see the model estate houses and the Estate Workshop dated 1922, a single-storey, granite ashlar building with wings at each end. A number of tollhouses with rounded ends can be seen along the road.

The bus takes a diversion towards Sauchen, passing the gateway to Cluny Castle, owned by the Gordons of Huntly. A Victorian Gothic house is hidden from the road. Back on the A944 you reach the Corrennie Forest stretching away to the north, and the granite quarries of Tillyfourie. The next place, Whitehouse, was once a station of the old Alford Valley Railway. The old track follows the line of the road from here to Alford where the ruined remains of the station can be seen. The single platform, the one-storey platform building and ruined sheds still exist.

Alford, the farming capital of the Howe of Alford, has a long straggling main street which developed in the 1850s. The old village lies round the church, two miles to the west. New houses have been built recently and the town has a pleasant air of community and prosperity. Montrose won a victory near here in 1645. Charles Murray, the north-east dialect poet lived here. His best-known volume *Hamewith* has been republished and is well worth looking for.

At the end of the street the road divides. If you are driving, first take the A980 to Craigievar Castle which stands on an impressive site on the eastern slope of the Hill of Craigievar. The land originally belonged to the Mortimer family (from the 15th century) and they are supposed to have begun building a castle at the end of the 16th century. But in 1610 it was acquired by William Forbes, a younger brother of Bishop Patrick Forbes of Aberdeen, who is alleged to have helped William with the costs of the castle. William himself was a Danzig merchant who completed the building in 1626. The castle is a six-storey, L-plan tower house, with corbelled turrets from the upper floors. The National Trust acquired the property in 1963.

Inside, the castle shows strong Renaissance influence, and its decorations and furnishings, so long in the hands of the Forbes and Forbes-Sempill family, give it the appearance still of a family home. The architect of the castle is generally supposed to be one, I. Bell, who remodelled Castle Fraser at about the same time. Nothing else is known of him. The most impressive room is the Great Hall. Architecturally it is a purely Gothic medieval structure, but the central groined vault is covered with Renaissance plasterwork, with medallion portraits of classical and biblical characters. At the lower end of the Hall are carved wooden screens, and the traditional minstrels' gallery has a Renaissance balustrade. Some of the bedrooms also have fine plaster decoration, and the motto 'Do not vaiken sleiping dogs' appears prominently.

Return to Alford and take the A944 again. (The

bus will take this route). Beyond the town the road makes a sharp turn over the Bridge of Alford, and the next few miles to Mossat Corner reveal some of the most beautiful scenery in Scotland. At Mossat the road bends sharply to the south, the A97. This is the bus route. To the west, just off the road stand the ruins of Kildrummy Castle. As Craigievar is perhaps the finest example of a Scottish tower house, so perhaps Kildrummy is the best surviving example of a 13th-century stone 'enceinte' castle. The position of the fortifications on a high rock with ravines on two sides is impressive. The castle was begun by Bishop Gilbert de Moravia, Bishop of Caithness from 1223-1245. Edward I came in 1296 and 1303 and commanded the building of an enormous gatehouse with two drum towers. It is modelled on the gatehouse at Harlech Castle, and it is also thought to be the work of the King's Master Builder, James St George.

The south-west curtain walls and the south tower are well-preserved. The chapel stands by the east wall, and the domestic buildings were ranged along the north wall. They consist of a Great Hall, with a kitchen and the lord's solar. On the highest part of the site is the Snow Tower, or donjon, much of which fell in 1806.

In 1306 the castle was besieged by Edward I, and Nigel Bruce, brother of Robert, was defeated. It also played a part in the Civil War, and in the Jacobite Rising of 1715, which the Earl of Mar, the owner of the castle, was supporting. After this, the castle was dismantled and used as a building quarry for the neighbourhood. In the last years of the 19th century, repairs and excavations were begun, and in 1951 the castle became the property of the Scottish Development Department. Colonel James Ogston began a new house on the opposite side of the ravine, and this is now a hotel. Below, the ravine has been landscaped with splendid gardens, which include Japanese and rock gardens, and some notable shrubs and trees.

Return to the road and continue towards Strathdon, the head of this part of the valley. You pass through the Glenbuchat Estate and over the Bridge of Buchat, where if you have time, you can walk up Glen Buchat, a pleasant walk in itself, to the old castle, now ruined. It was a Z-plan tower house, built in 1590 by John Gordon of Cairnburrow and his wife, Helen Carnegie. This date and the inscription 'Nothing on earth remanis bot fame', the latter now barely legible, can be seen over the doorway.

The most notable feature of the tower is that the two stair turrets are carried on 'trompes', or flying arches in French style, rather than on corbelling. It has been suggested that Helen Carnegie's father, Sir Robert Carnegie of Kinnaird, who had been sent on ambassadorial missions to the court of Henri II, may have met the French architect, Philibert de l'Orme, who used a similar device in the Tuileries. The Scottish Development Department also owns this monument, but has not been able to make it safe enough to explore completely.

The small village of Strathdon is the end of this route. The bus returns the same way, but by car it would be possible to continue along the A97, turning east along the B9119 to Tarland, and back to the city this way. Aberdeen to Strathdon and return is about 104 miles.

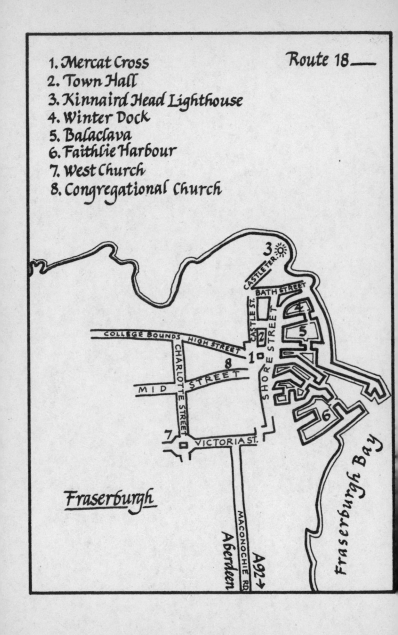

Route 18

1. Mercat Cross
2. Town Hall
3. Kinnaird Head Lighthouse
4. Winter Dock
5. Balaclava
6. Faithlie Harbour
7. West Church
8. Congregational Church

Fraserburgh

Fraserburgh Bay

Aberdeen

MACONOCHIE RD.

A92→

VICTORIA ST.

MID STREET

CHARLOTTE STREET

COLLEGE BOUNDS

HIGH STREET

SHORE STREET

CASTLE ST.

CASTLE TER.

BATH STREET

FRASERBURGH

THE FISHING PORTS OF THE NORTH-EAST OF Scotland, were active until recently with large catches. Lossiemouth, Buckie and Macduff in the north and Peterhead and Fraserburgh in the east are all worth visiting because they still have interesting buildings and harbour works. Peterhead has replaced its former fishing activities with oil-related industries, and the town has changed considerably. Fraserburgh to the north has replaced its herring industry with fish processing and canning. The town remains, albeit rather sadly, much as it was in former times.

Take a bus from Aberdeen along the A92, travelling over part of the route taken to Pitmedden and to Newburgh. The bus crosses the Ythan some fifteen miles north of Aberdeen at Ellon. The town was formerly the capital of Buchan, the north-east lowland region. The old bridge, built in 1783, can still be seen from its modern successor. Part of the 16th-century Ellon Castle in a landscaped garden by James Gordon (1706) lies to the north.

The road continues across a wide plain to the sea.

The countryside is less obviously picturesque than Deeside, or even Donside, but to its admirers it represents the triumph of man over his environment in the cultivation of every acre, the draining of marshland, the building of stone walls to enclose fields, and the unremitting struggle which goes on to the present day.

Fraserburgh developed round a castle built on Kinnaird Head. The rock stands 60 feet above the sea, and in 1574 Sir Alexander Fraser built a square machiolated tower, four storeys in height. The Commissioners of Northern Lighthouses used it as the base for the earliest lighthouse in the north of Scotland. In 1786-7 Thomas Smith built a short circular tower with a triangular-paned lantern, domed above on top of the tower. Single-storey keepers' cottages stand nearby.

The town is a good example of a burgh developed by an individual family. The reason for its founding is recorded in its first charter in 1546 which said, 'Whereas Alexander Fraser of Philorth for the convenience of his neighbours dwelling within the Sheriffdom of Aberdeen has built a harbour upon the sea shore within his lands of Faithlie in the Sheriffdom of Aberdeen in which ships and vessels overtaken by storms may be able to find refuge, both for the good service thus and otherwise rendered by the said Alexander . . . (we) erect the town of Faithlie into a free borough of barony'.

The grandson of this Alexander, also Alexander, built the castle, expanded the harbour, and even built a University in 1595. This institution did not succeed and although some building was begun nothing remains except the name College Bounds at the north end of the town. It has attractive one- and two-storey granite houses. At this end of the town also is the cove called Broadsea Shore. Broadsea and Faithlie, mentioned in the charter, were two small fishing villages assimilated into the town of Fraserburgh.

Walk along College Bounds to the High Street and follow this until you reach Saltoun Square. In the centre there is a Mercat Cross, standing 17 feet high. It was placed on the present base in 1850, but the cross itself bears the date 1736 and the initials LAS (Lord Alexander Saltoun, the title of the Fraser family). The Fraser Arms and the Royal Arms are also inscribed. The parish church to the north-east of the square was rebuilt in 1802, but much restored again later. Next to it is the Fraser Mausoleum, a curious stepped, pyramidal building. The classical-style Town House is rather cramped on its corner. As Pratt wrote in his famous book on Buchan, it has 'a domical sphere of good design, but situated too near the parish church to show to advantage'. Opposite stands the old inn, the Saltoun Arms.

Leave the square through a shopping precinct at the north corner. Walk along Castle Street and Castle Terrace and you will see the Kinnaird Head Lighthouse. Nearby is the Kinnaird Head Fish Canning Works, built in 1863. The boatbuilding yard, a large corrugated iron shed with single-storey workshops, was built in the last century.

Return along Bath Street and Shore Street. Here

you can see the harbour basins, starting with the Winter Dock, the Balaclava, the three basins which link to the outer harbour, and the Faithlie Harbour. The first haven was built in 1576, but the present complex harbour dates from the first years of the 19th century, with the long breakwater completed in the second half of the same century.

Many of the houses at the north end of Shore Street, behind the church and the Town Hall, have been rebuilt in a sympathetic project which fits in well with the older granite cottages. At the end of Shore Street is the old Fraserburgh Station, originally built in 1865 by the Formantine and Buchan Railway, but extensively rebuilt later. The entrance is a single-storey granite ashlar building with crow-stepped gables.

Walk back past the South Church in Seaforth Street, and then westwards along Victoria Street. The grid pattern of the streets of the town will then be apparent. The West Church stands in the centre of the cross-roads. Then walk north along Charlotte Street and then east along Mid Street looking at the solid granite buildings. The Congregational Church, an early 19th-century building, stands on the north side of Mid Street. Fraserburgh Academy, founded in 1872 by John Park, a merchant, has moved from its site in the same street.

The south of the town has been developed for tourism with putting and bowling greens, a caravan site, bathing facilities and a golf-course.

Route 19

1. Castle
2. Cathedral
3. Cooper Park
4. Little Cross
5. Elgin Museum
6. Kirk
7. Muckle Cross
8. Site of Thunderton House
9. Gray's Hospital
10. Civic Offices
11. Railway Station

ELGIN

River Lossie

HIGH STREET

SOUTH STREET

A96 Aberdeen

ELGIN

ELGIN IS A JOURNEY OF JUST UNDER TWO
hours by train from Aberdeen. It is possible to go by
bus, but this takes much longer. The train goes
through Inverurie, Insch, Huntly and Keith, and
passes through lovely countryside. On the early-
morning train which leaves Aberdeen at 7.36 am
you can often see herons, pheasants and wildfowl
along the route.

Elgin is a royal burgh and, although it is a town of
fewer than 17,000 inhabitants, it gives the impression of being a prosperous community with a very
strong identity. The town lies on an east-west ridge
above the River Lossie which flows on the northern
side. The backbone of the town is one long street,
the High Street, which follows this ridge from the
ruins of the castle on Lady Hill, so named after the
chapel in the fortress, to the Cathedral at the east
end. Residential streets with houses built in the
19th and 20th centuries now stretch beyond this
main street, but it remains the centre of the town.

David I (1124-1153) granted Elgin its first charter
and established the town as a royal stronghold. In
1224 the Bishopric of Moray was moved here from

Spynie. Elgin was the subject of many attacks from the north, the most notorious of which was made by Alexander Stuart, Earl of Buchan, a son of Robert II, known as 'the Wolf of Badenoch', who sacked the town in 1390 and burnt the Cathedral as the rhyme records.

Brynt the kirk was of Elgyne
Be wyld wykkyd heiland men

The castle was destroyed in the 16th century and never restored.

The Cathedral at the other end of the town was built in the course of the 13th century. The central tower was restored after the burning in 1390. Part of it fell again in 1506. This was restored again, but after the Reformation the Cathedral was allowed to fall into disrepair. The lead was removed from its roof in 1567 and the central tower collapsed again in 1711, and the whole place became a quarry for building material. The Chapter House survived because it was used by the Incorporated Trades as a meeting-place. The ruins were acquired as an Ancient Monument, and much work has been done in the past decade by the Scottish Development Department to prevent further decay.

The West Front of the Cathedral has two towers with elongated buttresses in early pointed style. They were of four storeys (90 ft high) and originally had lead-covered, wooden spires. The great West Door is richly decorated with dog-tooth and trefoil patterns. The inner screen of the door was destroyed in the fire of 1390 and replaced by a later version. The empty panel over the door once contained a carved representation of the Holy

Trinity the dedication of the Cathedral. The great window above also dates from after the fire and is decorated with elaborate tracery.

Inside the Cathedral you can still see the traces of burning on the inside wall of the west end. Here there are decorations with human heads, owls and leaves. The nave had twelve pillars, six on each side. There were chapels against the outer walls on the north and south sides. These are the oldest parts of the building. The northern aisle once contained a chapel dedicated to St Thomas à Becket, and the south two chapels to St Peter and St Paul. All this is now at ground level. Parts of the north and south transepts remain. The tower, as has been explained, was rebuilt in the early 15th century. A statue of Bishop Innes (1407-1414), who began this restoration, once stood on the tower, but now stands on the ground.

The extension of the south transept has strong vertical buttresses. The lower storey has lancet windows with round-headed ones in the clerestory. The gable also had lancet windows but these no longer remain. The doorway is at the south-west with an oval window above. The north transept is similar in design. A rood screen marked off the nave from the choir. To the north was St Columba's Aisle leading to the Chapter House, an octagonal building with a central pillar of stone built after 1390, and rib-and-panel vaulting decorated with carved bosses, some with leaves and flowers, some with grotesque human heads, others with shields with holy symbols such as the Five Wounds, and one figure, a Christ in Majesty. The 17th-century tombs were brought here from St Giles' Parish Kirk in 1826. The windows are traceried and their corbels are again carved with figures such as a fox dressed as a friar.

The choir contained oak stalls for the canons with the Bishop's Throne at the east end. The presbytery is late 13th-century pointed Gothic with windows in the east gable, side windows and a clerestory. There are consecration crosses on the walls. The South Aisle, called St Mary's Aisle, has the tomb of Bishop Winchester (1436-1460), Bishop Tulloch (1471-82), an effigy in an arched recess, and tombs of the Gordons of Huntly. This aisle is better-preserved and has rib-and-panel vaulting. Here again are splendid carved bosses with dragons and foliage.

The graveyard has a number of interesting tombs with fine inscriptions. Look at the one to the family of John Geddes, 1687, with the verse:

This world is a cite full of streets
And death is the mercat that all men meets.
If lyfe were a thing that monie could buy
The poor could not live and the rich would not
die.

Near the Cathedral precincts are the remains of the Chanonry, the Canons' College, now called the Bishop's Palace. (The Bishop actually had his residence at the older ecclesiastical site of Spynie.) This building, dated 1557, has a square staircase tower and two wings. To the south-east, by the riverbank, is the old Water Yett, one of the old gateways to the city. Cooper Park lies to the west of the Cathedral, and the Public Library Building in it

144

was formerly the 18th-century town house of the Grant family, Grant Lodge.

Return again to the High Street. To the south of the Cathedral stands the Little Cross, 15 feet high with a slender sandstone shaft, approached by four circular steps. It is surmounted with an Ionic capital and a sundial dated 1733. It is generally assumed to mark the boundary of the jurisdiction of Burgh and Cathedral. No 1 High Street is the Elgin Museum, a classical building of 1842, which houses a good collection of local records. Nearby is Duff of Dipple's Banking House with three arcades. It has richly-carved dormer windows and the initials ID and MI. Walking westwards you come to the church in the centre of the road. The original parish church was damaged by the Wolf of Badenoch, and it was further diminished in the 17th century by the removal of its transepts when the road was widened. Finally the whole of the 'Muckle Kirk' was taken down in 1826 and Archibald Simpson was commissioned to build a new church. The result was one of his finest buildings. The design was a Greek Doric temple with a portico of six fluted columns at the west end, and a tower at the east. The upper part of the tower was adapted from the Choragic Monument of Lysicrates in Athens, The church with its commanding site dominates the High Street. The Muckle Cross is a copy of an earlier one.

On the south side of the High Street, a little further on, in Thunderton Place, is the former Thunderton House, a 17th-century town house which belonged successively to the Moray, Duffus and Dunbar families, and is now a hotel. It was considerably altered in the last century, and its tower destroyed.

At the far western end of the High Street is the domed Gray's Hospital. It was endowed by an East India merchant, Dr Alexander Gray (1751-1808), for the indigent sick of the town, and was designed by Gillespie Graham. The buildings are now used as a modern hospital.

Walk back along South Street, parallel to the High Street on the south side of the town. Northfield House, the 18th-century town house of the Dunbars after they left Thunderton House, now provides the Civic Offices. The old buildings of Elgin Academy, notably the classical block added in 1800, stand here. The school itself has moved further out. At the east end of this street the names of Greyfriars and Abbey Street reveal an earlier religious foundation. The Convent of Mercy occupies the site of the old Greyfriars' monastery. Hardly anything remains of the original.

Walk back to the station along one of the streets of pleasant late 19th-century and early 20th-century houses. The station itself has its main offices on the down side in a two-storey granite ashlar building with an attic, which was rebuilt in 1902 by the Great North of Scotland Railway.

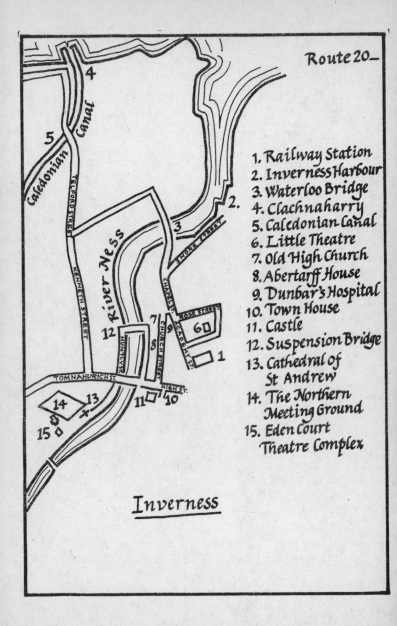

1. Railway Station
2. Inverness Harbour
3. Waterloo Bridge
4. Clachnaharry
5. Caledonian Canal
6. Little Theatre
7. Old High Church
8. Abertarff House
9. Dunbar's Hospital
10. Town House
11. Castle
12. Suspension Bridge
13. Cathedral of
   St Andrew
14. The Northern
   Meeting Ground
15. Eden Court
   Theatre Complex

Inverness

INVERNESS

INVERNESS IS THE LARGEST TOWN NORTH
of Aberdeen, and it is the centre of the Highland
Region. It lies on the River Ness, is linked with the
Moray Firth, and by land and air joins north and
south. You can reach it by train from Aberdeen; the
journey takes about two and a half hours. Beyond
Elgin, already described in the previous route, the
train goes through Forres and Nairn to Inverness.
For the last part of the journey the line follows the
Moray Firth.

The town, because of its important geographical
position, has evidences of settlement from an early
period. David I (1124-1153) gave it a charter as a
royal burgh, and William the Lion fortified the
town. In recent years Inverness' position as capital
of the Highlands has increased its importance as
the home of the Highlands and Islands Board and
its associated enterprises.

Inverness Station, opened in 1855 by the
Inverness and Nairn Railway, has been extensively
rebuilt in recent years. It links the lines from
Aberdeen, from Perth and to the North. Come out
of the station and turn north-west along Academy

Street to Chapel Street and Shore Street. This brings you to the River Ness and its quays. These constitute what is called Inverness Harbour, and they were the work, from 1847 on, of the engineer Joseph Mitchell. On the east bank there are small one- and two-storey warehouses. From the west bank cross by the late 19th-century Waterloo Bridge, a five-span road bridge, to Grant Street, then join the A9 which leads to the beginning of the Caledonian Canal. Clachnaharry village contains 19th-century cottages, most of which are single-storey and were built for the workers on the canal. The Clachnaharry Bridge was rebuilt in 1909 for the Highland Railway and is a steel-girder swing bridge. There are two old distilleries nearby, the Glenalbye Distillery, rebuilt from a mill in 1884, and the Glenmhor Distillery, built in 1892.

The Caledonian Canal begins here and you can see the basin and first lochs. The work of Thomas Telford, it was built between 1803 and 1822, and links the North Sea and the Atlantic, covering 60 miles. In summer it is possible to take a steamer trip to Loch Ness from here.

Return to the east bank of the Ness, going back to the centre of the town. Notice in Rose Street the late 19th-century foundry, famous engineering shops. The main block faces the street and has three gables with an elliptically-arched doorway. Back in Academy Street, once the site of the Inverness Academy which has now moved to another site, the 1840 classical buildings of Dr Andrew Bell's School, later the Farraline Park School, are reached along Strother's Lane. They now house the Little Theatre. Across Academy Street you reach a large complex of covered markets.

Go through the market to reach Church Street, where Inverness' best-preserved historic buildings remain. Halfway along on the riverside is the Old High Church, standing on St Michael's Mound. It is alleged to be the site of a church founded by St Columba's mission in 565. By the 12th century there was certainly a church there dedicated to St Mary the Virgin. The 14th-century vaulted tower remains. The old church was replaced by the present building in 1769. Two stones by the West Door (in the churchyard) are pointed out as marking the place of execution of two prisoners taken after The Battle of Culloden. Inside there is a central pulpit and a gallery for the Council to sit in. The kirkyard has interesting tombs, including an ornate burial area for the Robertsons of Inshes.

Other churches in the street are St Columba High, extended in 1866 with a steeple, and the Free Greyfriars Church which holds Gaelic services. The place names Friars Lane and Street mark the area once owned by the Dominicans or Black Friars who founded a monastery here in 1233 which remained until the Reformation.

Church Street also contains a number of interesting secular buildings. Abertarff House was restored in 1966 by the National Trust. It is a late-16th-century, whitewashed house on an L-shaped plan with crow-stepped gables. A square watchtower springs from the stair tower. It is now used as the headquarters of *An Comunn*

Gaidhealach, the Gaelic movement. The 17th-century Dunbar Hospital is across the street. It has seven dormer windows and crow-stepped gables, and was built in 1688 by Provost Alexander Dunbar for the poor and aged. It is satisfactory to record that it is still used as a Centre for the Elderly.

Walk down Church Street in a south-westerly direction and you will see at the junction with the High Street, the Town House, a late-19th-century flamboyant Gothic building (1878). In 1921 Lloyd George held a Cabinet Meeting here, the first to be held outside London. The Mercat Cross is an early-20th-century copy of an earlier one. Beside it is a stone, the Stone of Tubs, *Clach na Cudainn,* where women were supposed to have rested their buckets on the way to the river. This stone has the legend attached to it that Inverness will last as long as the stone survives.

Continue along Castle Wynd and climb Castle Hill. The castle, where the Sheriff Court sits, is an impressive 19th-century building, designed by William Burn in 1835. The castle well and old courtyard are all that survive of earlier structures.

Cross the river again by the Suspension Bridge, a triple-span structure built in 1961 to replace an earlier one built in 1849. Walk southwards on the riverbank along Huntly Street. The Cathedral of St Andrew, a decorated Gothic building of 1869-94, is the Episcopal Church of the Bishop of Moray, Ross and Caithness. The Northern Meeting Ground has held the Highland Games, and to the west of this open area is the Eden Court Theatre and Restaurant, a splendid enterprise of the 1970s, which has given Inverness a well-deserved reputation as a centre for theatre and ballet.

Inverness is an attractive town and an excellent centre for the exploration of the Highlands.

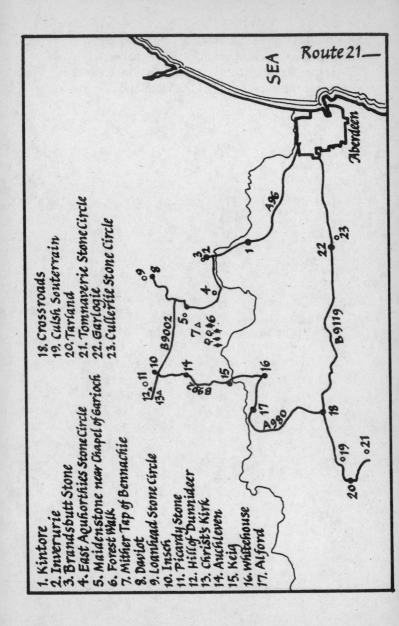

SEA

Aberdeen

A96

B9002

B9119

A980

1. Kintore
2. Inverurie
3. Brandsbutt Stone
4. East Aquhorthies Stone Circle
5. Maidenstone near Chapel of Garioch
6. Forest Walk
7. Mither Tap of Bennachie
8. Dawlot
9. Loanhead Stone Circle
10. Insch
11. Picardy Stone
12. Hill of Dunnideer
13. Christ's Kirk
14. Auchleven
15. Keig
16. Whitehouse
17. Alford
18. Crossroads
19. Culsh Souterrain
20. Tarland
21. Tomnaverie Stone Circle
22. Garlogie
23. Cullerlie Stone Circle

Route 21

PREHISTORIC SITES

THE LAST THREE ROUTES IN THIS BOOK ARE only possible by car. Take stout boots with you because some of the sites are off the beaten track, in fields and on hilltops.

The North-east of Scotland is particularly well-endowed with prehistoric sites. A rough guide for getting them into perspective is:

> 10000 to 4000 BC Mesolithic or Middle Stone Age
> 4000 to 2000 BC Neolithic or New Stone Age
> 2000 to 1000 BC Bronze Age
> c700 BC to c400 AD Iron Age

The Romans also reached the area and sites of battles are recorded, but there is little to see.

Leave Aberdeen by the A96 to Kintore. Just south-west of the village is the site of a Roman camp which has not been excavated. Continue on the A96 to Inverurie where stands the Pictish stone by the Bass, already mentioned in an earlier route. If you have time, look first at the Brandsbutt Stone which stands to the north-west on the A96 about one mile beyond the town centre. It has Pictish symbols and an inscription in the early writing, ogham.

If you want to get on more quickly do not enter the town, but instead turn sharply to the left just after crossing the river. Drive until you reach the signpost for East Aquhorthies farm. From here a rough track leads to the site of a recumbent stone circle, which takes its name from the farm. These circles are a particular feature of Aberdeenshire and probably date from the Bronze Age. They consist of a ring of standing stones with two upright stones within the circle. A recumbent stone lies lengthways between the two uprights. They are assumed to have served ritual purposes, although there has been speculation in recent years about a possible astrological significance. The East Aquhorthies group is well-preserved, and consists of nine standing stones outside in a circle of 63½ feet in diameter, and the inner group is intact. There are traces of a few other stones. The site is owned by the Scottish Development Department and is accessible at all times without charge.

Return to the road and continue on to Chapel of Garioch (pronounced 'Gairie') and turn left at the cross-roads. About one and a half miles along this minor road is the Maidenstone, probably dating from the ninth century AD. It is perhaps the best-known early Christian monument in Aberdeenshire. One side depicts an elaborate Celtic Cross and on the other side are Pictish symbols of comb and mirror. This monument is accessible at all times without charge.

It is possible to walk south from here (part of the way on a Forest Walk) and see in the distance—or climb the 1700 feet if you have the energy—the

Mither Tap of Bennachie, one of the six peaks of the range. On the top there is an Iron Age stone fort, about 700 feet in circumference, with massive walls which still survive.

Return to Chapel of Garioch, and just through the hamlet, take the road to the left, north to the A96. Cross the road and take the minor road to Daviot. About half a mile beyond this village is Loanhead Recumbent Stone Circle. This has been dated to c 1800-1600 BC, but also shows signs of long occupation. The circle is 66 feet in diameter, and an enormous recumbent stone stretches across the middle. The site was excavated in 1934 and several small cairns were discovered. The cist below one of these revealed pottery from the Middle to the Late Bronze Age, and also Iron Age artefacts. The hearth found in the ring cairn within the circle suggests that the site was used by later generations to live in.

Return through Daviot to the A96 and drive along it towards Insch. At Mill of Carden turn west along the B9002, then turn off on to the B992 through the town of Insch. Take the second turn northwards, and about two miles along the road you will see, on the left, the Picardy Stone (7th-8th century AD), one of the oldest Pictish stones, with deeply-incised symbols, a serpent, mirror, and 'spectacles'. This stone is always accessible free of charge.

Go back to Insch and rejoin the B9002 going northwards. A mile further on, there are sites on both sides of the road. To the north on the Hill of Dunnideer you can see the ruin of a 13th-century castle of the Balliols, and surrounding it the remains of an earth rampart and of an Iron Age fort. A number of Iron Age forts in the north-east of Scotland are known as 'vitrified' forts. They were built with timbers lining stone walls, and when they caught fire, the heat 'vitrified' the stones into a firm bond. Whether this was done by the inhabitants' enemies, or by the inhabitants themselves to make their forts stronger, is a matter of doubt. Some pre-historians dislike both theories, but have not produced another explanation. On the south side of the road, the hill, Christ's Kirk, marks the site of a deserted village (not excavated).

Return to Insch and just before the station, turn south along the B992 through Auchleven and Keig to Whitehouse. Turn west onto the A944 through Alford, and then take the A980 for about 10 miles to the cross-roads formed with the B9119. Turn west along this road towards Tarland. One and a half miles before the village, on the south side of the road, you can see Culsh Souterrain. These earth houses date from the Iron Age, and were underground chambers. This one is well-preserved, and still has its roof stones. You need a torch to look inside. The site belongs to the Scottish Development Department and is always accessible.

Continue through Tarland to the junction with the B9094. Turn east on this road, and less than a mile along it to the south is the Tomnaverie Recumbent Stone Circle. This differs from the other two at East Aquhorthies and Loanhead in its hilltop site and in its having two rings of standing stones. The recumbent stone is 11 feet long. The site has been dated to the Bronze Age. It also belongs to the Scottish Development Department and is accessible at all times.

Return to Tarland and drive along the B9119 eastwards towards Aberdeen. Just before Roadside of Garlogie, turn south along the B9125, and take the first turn on the left. Less than a mile along the road is Cullerlie Stone Circle. It dates from the Bronze Age and consists of eight stones no longer upright. The burial cairns within the circle are of a later period. (Scottish Development Department, open at all times.)

Go back to the B9119 and drive the ten miles back to Aberdeen. This is a long day's expedition and is best undertaken in the summer when the long days and better weather conditions make the hill climbs easier.

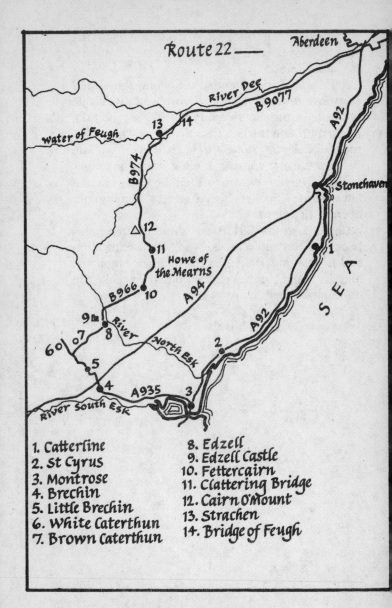

Route 22 ——

1. Catterline
2. St Cyrus
3. Montrose
4. Brechin
5. Little Brechin
6. White Caterthun
7. Brown Caterthun
8. Edzell
9. Edzell Castle
10. Fettercairn
11. Clattering Bridge
12. Cairn O'Mount
13. Strachen
14. Bridge of Feugh

SOUTH FROM ABERDEEN

THIS ROUTE EXPLORES THE COAST BEYOND Dunnottar to Montrose, then turns inland to Brechin, into the Howe of the Mearns and back over the dramatic Cairn O'Mount, returning to Aberdeen along the South Deeside road.

Leave Aberdeen on the A92 through Stonehaven (see Route 11). On the other side of the town continue along the A92, the coast road past Dunnottar. About nine miles south, turn off eastwards to the small fishing village of Catterline. It became famous after World War II when a number of Glasgow artists, most notably Joan Eardley (1921-1963) whose portraits of Glasgow children and whose landscapes hang in many galleries in Scotland and beyond, made their homes here.

Return to the A92, and just over 20 miles to the south you reach St Cyrus, a beach and dune Nature Reserve of 227 acres which stretches to the point where the North Esk river flows into the sea. You can follow a Nature Trail of one and a half miles to look at the 300 different plants that have been recorded here. Less industriously, you can wander among the tombs in the old kirkyard on the shore, with their hourglasses to mark the transitoriness of life, the skulls and crossbones, and one 17th-century stone showing a husband and wife both struck by the spear of Death. There are also ruins of two small chapels.

Leaving St Cyrus, continue on the A92 for about nine miles to Montrose, a splendid town, whose most dramatic natural feature is a large tidal basin which receives the waters of the South Esk river. The basin is impressive both at high-water, and also at low-tide when the mudflats are covered with birds. The church (built 1791) in the High Street has two tiers of galleries. Its church tower and steeple with a spire of over 200 feet were added in 1832 by the architect, Gillespie Graham. Its churchyard, too, has interesting gravestones. The old Town House, just north in the same street, dates from 1763 with an early 19th-century arcade. The statue is of Sir Robert Peel.

Many of the houses in Montrose are gable-ended, and it is worth looking down some of the alleyways at them. To the east side of the town in Panmure Place is the classical and golden-domed Montrose Academy (1815). The school, founded in 1534 by John Erskine of Dun, was the first in Scotland to teach Greek. The Museum and Art Gallery, almost facing it, is worth visiting. It has a wide collection ranging from Pictish stones to modern art, and also items of local interest from semi-precious stones to arms, coins and books.

The port lies to the south-east and is interesting on account of its warehouses and boatyards and the

Customs House. James Graham, Marquess of Montrose (1612-1650), is perhaps the town's best known son, although he was probably born at Old Montrose, a few miles to the south-west, Andrew Melville (1545-1622) and Joseph Hume (1777-1855) pay tribute to Montrose's educational eminence.

Leave the town by the A935 and continue to Brechin, which ranks as a city because it is the seat of a bishopric. The Bishop no longer lives here, but the Cathedral remains. The foundation was Celtic, but the present church dates from the 13th and 14th centuries. It was rebuilt in 1806 and restored again in the early 20th century. The crenellated tower with its 58 feet-high stone spire dates from the 14th century. The carved West Door and the window above are worth attention. Perhaps the most notable feature is the Celtic Round Tower, 87 feet high, and dating from the 9th century. Over the lintel of the doorway, above the ground for safety, there is a figure of Christ Crucified. The Bishop's Palace no longer remains. The rest of the town's buildings, mostly of red sandstone, are not out-standing as architecture, although the 1838 Mechanics' Institute at the west end of the town has great panache.

Brechin is the gateway to the Mearns. Leave the town by the minor road to Little Brechin, and continue on it for about five miles until you come to a parking place. From here it is possible to climb two hills with interesting forts on their summits. The southern one, White Caterthun, is perhaps the more rewarding. The Iron Age fort is almost two acres in area and is enclosed with two banks and a ditch. Inside the enclosure are two stone walls, the inner of about 40 feet thick and the outer about half that width. The northern hill, Brown Caterthun, has six rings or fortifications, less well-preserved. Both sites belong to the Scottish Development Department and are always accessible. Return along the same minor road for just over a mile, and then turn north-east at the cross-roads to Edzell.

Beyond the village on the Glen Lethnot road, notice the 17th-century dovecot at Mains of Edzell Farm, and then the ruins of the Castle. Built in red sandstone, it dates from the 16th century. You go in at the east wall and see the Tower House with a fine Great Hall on the first floor. The ruins of other buildings also remain. Most impressive, however, is the Pleasance, the formal garden conceived in the first years of the 17th century by Sir David Lindsay, Lord Edzell. His coat of arms and the date 1604 appear on a doorway in the north-east corner. The walls depict in bas-relief in German style, the Cardinal Virtues (west wall), the Liberal Arts (south wall) and the Planetary Deities (east wall). Plants grow in the walls and in the formal parterres. The family motto 'Dum Spiro Spero' (While I breathe I hope) is spelled out in box hedging. Also of interest are the Summer House at the east corner, and the Foundations of the Bath House.

Return to Edzell village and take the B966 to Fettercairn. The redstone archway commemorates a visit by Queen Victoria in 1861. Turn north along the B974, the road over the Cairn O'Mount. This road should only be attempted in good weather, because it is one of the first to become impassable in snow. The road follows the valley to Clattering Bridge, and then rises steeply to the summit of 1475 feet. The view from the top is one of the most magnificent in the region. Continue along the road through Strachen and Bridge of Feugh, and return to Aberdeen along the south side of the Dee.

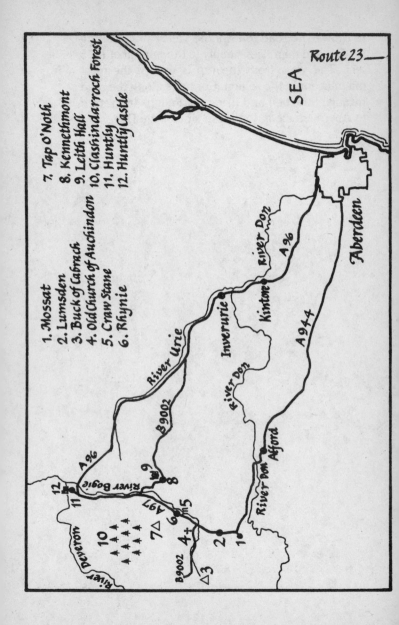

SEA

Aberdeen

1. Mossat
2. Lumsden
3. Buck of Cabrach
4. Old Church of Auchindoir
5. Craw Stane
6. Rhynie
7. Tap O'Noth
8. Kennethmont
9. Leith Hall
10. Clashindarroch Forest
11. Huntly
12. Huntly Castle

River Urie

River Don

River Bogie

River Deveron

River Don

Inverurie

Kintore

Alford

A96

A944

A96

A97

B9002

B9002

MOSSAT TO HUNTLY

FOLLOW THE DONSIDE ROUTE TO MOSSAT Corner, then continue on the A97 through Lumsden, planned in 1840 by the Lumsdens of Clova. The long main street has a green at one end, and the village looks south to the Buck of Cabrach (2368 ft). The Old Bakery at the further end of the village on the north side has been taken over by the sculptor, Fred Bushe, who runs the Scottish Sculpture Workshop. Stop and look at the work he and his colleagues have on view.

Follow the same road towards Rhynie. About three miles further on, turn on to the B9002 to look at the Old Church of Auchindoin. The building, St Mary's, is a ruined 13th-century parish church. It has a Transitional door with dog-tooth decoration and a lancet window in the north wall. The belfry dates from 1664. The church's most famous feature is the 16th-century sacrament house with a cross and holy water stoup. The kirkyard has interesting tombstones.

Return to the A97 and continue to Rhynie. Just under a mile before the village on the right-hand side of the road you can see the Craw Stane, a Celtic monument with a Christian fish symbol among its decorations.

The village of Rhynie is built round a green which itself has four old stones on it, probably all that remains of a stone circle. Look north-east to the Tap O'Noth (1851 ft) on which is a vitrified fort with a high rampart remaining. The A941 which leaves the village on the east side goes to Cabrach and on to Dufftown, and skirts part of Clashindarroch Forest, the largest Forestry Commission plantation in the region.

Follow the A97 for 5½ miles and then take the A979 towards Kennethmont Station. On the left a fine avenue leads to Leith Hall, now owned by the National Trust. The Leiths were a family who came from Edinburgh to trade in Aberdeen, where they were established by the 14th century. In 1649 one member of the family, James Leith of Barns, built a small country house on the present site. It was a single rectangular building with small corbelled towers at roof level and now forms the north sector of the courtyard.

The mid-18th century saw the family's fortunes increase with the acquisition of Hay lands. In the 1750s more building of stables and domestic offices was begun and 40 years later, a Palladian-style block with pavilions at the sides and Venetian windows with classical-style pediments above them. Local materials were used, for example harled walls, but the effect is very attractive. The west side of the courtyard was enclosed in 1868.

The Leith-Hays always supported the Jacobite

cause, so the house contains mementoes of this period, as well as the furniture and the collection of glass and porcelain which the family acquired.

Go back to the A97 and drive towards Huntly. This stretch of the road is Strathbogie, with the River Bogie to the east and another part of Clashindarroch Forest stretching away on the high ground. As you go into the town of Huntly notice the three-arched bridge over the River Bogie.

Huntly lies in the bowl of the wooded hills where the rivers Bogie and Deveron meet. The town was the centre of power for the Gordon clan and became a borough of barony for the family in 1545. Huntly is built on a rectangular plan with a fine square in the centre. The Museum here is worth looking at. The names of the streets reflect the patronage of the Gordon family.

Duke Street has a plaque to George Macdonald (1824-1905). He is best-known in Britain today as the author of children's books, such as *At the Back of the North Wind* and *The Princess and Curdie*, but he also wrote novels with a local setting and mystical works like *Lilith*. His use of myth and allegory has made him something of a cult figure in the United States, where there is a flourishing George Macdonald Society.

Architecturally, the most important buildings in the town, apart from the castle, are those of the Gordon Schools. The fifth Duchess of Huntly employed Archibald Simpson to build them as a memorial to her husband. He designed a two-storey double E-plan building in Jacobean style. The front is faced with sandstone ashlar and has a central pend arch with an octagonal clock tower, ogee-shaped at the top. The building was carefully modernised in the early 1970s.

Huntly Castle, now ruined, stands at the end of an avenue to the north of the town. The strategic importance of the site at the confluence of two rivers and two important roads is clear. The motte of the Norman castle can still be seen. The bailey of this early fortification later (probably at the turn of the 14th century) received an L-shaped stone keep, and in the course of the civil wars of the 15th century the Earls of Huntly extended the stone buildings. The underground basement and the dungeon of the round tower remain from this period.

In the 16th century the fourth Earl rebuilt the part known as the 'palace', but this in its turn was destroyed when the fifth Earl rebelled. In 1597 he was reconciled with the king and two years later was made first Marquess of Huntly. He restored the castle by 1602, creating a splendid Renaissance-style palace. The first-floor windows are modelled on those at Blois, which he had seen while in exile in France.

There are five heraldic decorations notably over the great door which has the arms of the first Marquess and his wife and the royal arms of James VI and I and his queen, Anne of Denmark. The fireplace in the Great Hall has similar coats of arms and the inscriptions:

Sen God doth vs defend
Ve sal prevail vpto the end.
and
To thaes that love God
al thingis virkis to the best.

The palace stands to roof height, but much of the rest of the castle was allowed to fall into ruin after the Gordons left it in the mid-18th century. The building is now in the care of the Scottish Development Department.

Return to Aberdeen either by the A97 or on the A96 through Inverurie and Kintore.